DESIGNS FOR LIVING

A Conversation with Paul Goldberger, Roger Seifter,
Randy Correll, Grant Marani, and Gary Brewer

PAUL GOLDBERGER You have all done very serious work and have resumes that are long and distinguished, as well as reputations of your own. And you've all chosen to work for a firm that has someone else's name on the door. Does that ever enter into your thinking? Now that the office has grown, is RAMSA viewed as a brand like SOM? How do you, as people who are not named Robert A. M. Stern, fit in?

GRANT MARANI To give this discussion some perspective, we've all been with Bob for about 30 years—except for Gary.

GARY BREWER I've been here since 1989.

PG That says a great deal that the newcomer has been here for 24 years.

GM When we first started, it was absolutely Bob Stern's firm. Over the years, each of us has in some way been identified by individual clients who come to us, not necessarily for Bob; I think we can say that now. But Bob's name is still on the door and that's the umbrella we work under, and we all feel comfortable with that.

PG One of the goals of this book is to explore that and what it means.

ROGER SEIFTER The name on the door signifies a level of quality to our clients and prospective clients, which to some extent transcends individuals. We've each been able to leverage that so we're able to do work here that we might not have if we were sole practitioners or at other firms. The house projects we do are very special.

PG That puts it very well: being at RAMSA allows you the advantages of the name as a symbol of quality that attracts and reassures clients, yet you're able to work very much on your own. In many ways you have the freedom you would have if you had your own practice.

RANDY CORRELL Here, we're always part of a something bigger; we have opportunities afforded us that those who have left can't attain. Each of us, at least once if not twenty times over the last thirty years, has wondered if we wouldn't have been better off on our own. Certainly many people who started here have gone off on their own. Some of them are my friends, and I look at what they do and I look at what I do and compare: people who have smaller firms often get stuck doing one thing or in one place. For example, not only does the firm work with clients who come in for houses, but we also have clients who ask us to design apartment buildings. RAMSA has done quite a number of buildings where one of us was subsequently hired to design apartments or penthouses. And we've had house clients who then hired RAMSA to build corporate headquarters. It's beyond just a name: we're part of something bigger, more interesting, more varied. We're collaborating with a team of colleagues who are involved in all sorts of architectural endeavors, not just colleagues who go out to see Mr. Smith and Mrs. Jones to visit their apartment or their house.

GB I would add that Bob Stern is involved with every house—in fact with every project in the office, not just the residences—and it's nice to have someone who is one step away from the project who acts as an outside critic.

PG That invites my next question: how engaged is Bob Stern in most projects? I ask knowing it must vary to some extent from project to project.

GB This conversation is very interesting because it hardly ever gets written about. I don't know if you read Mosette Broderick's *Triumvirate: McKim, Mead & White,* which starts to get into how the firm worked beyond just the three name partners. I would say the high quality of our firm's work is a function of how the office is structured: with 300-plus people, you can't have one lead design partner who designs everything from the concept to the profiles. Bob is involved in every project, but with the house partners, there's a level of trust. Bob is involved at the beginning, but he's not interested in conversations about how somebody's walk-in closet is laid out. That's an important part of getting a house done right, but he knows he can trust us with decisions large and small.

GM To add to Gary's point, we use Bob as a sounding board for our ideas. When we start a project, we come up with a number of ideas for the particular site and program based on discussions with the clients, and then we talk those through with Bob. He might say, "This is really good; why don't you try this or that?" We use him as our critic. He helps with the initial ideas; sometimes he'll just leave us alone for the rest of the project and sometimes he'll be more involved. If it's a site that has certain challenges that stimulate him intellectually, he'll get more involved.

RS Bob doesn't have time, and I think he's realized he may not have the interest in the details that he once did. The design of a house or apartment is necessarily a very hands-on process. For the design to work well as architecture and for it to work well for the client, our clients want someone who is very senior involved every step of the way. You need a certain mentality to be able to do that over and over again. Each of us has that so Bob's able to step back and let us do it.

PG Your reputation is that you're a firm that accepts conventions and then elevates them, making something that aspires to be more ambitious perhaps, but not fundamentally different from what is familiar to everyone. Your work never appears to start with the premise that we need to reinvent the idea of "house." You build on precedent, but in an intelligent way. And you each work in a range of styles. How do you make a decision about what style is right for a particular house? Do clients come to you and say, "I want a Georgian house or a Spanish Mediterranean house?"

RS Sometimes they do and sometimes they don't. With clients who don't have an idea of what they want, we'll put together a style book—a book of precedents with nice color photographs, arranged by style—so that they and we can understand what they like. Typically when we decide on a style for a house, we choose one that's appropriate for the place where we're building.

GB Clients who want traditional American houses typically want regional styles. They know a place like East Hampton or Bel Air or Santa Barbara, and they're drawn to the character that the architecture gives to the places where they've chosen to build. If you look at our portfolio, or those of other traditional architects practicing today, you'll see a limited range of styles. No one's coming to us for a Gilded Age mansion. There are lots of traditional styles that people don't consider acceptable these days.

PG The firm has always emphasized a sense of place. That is key. You're not likely to build a shingle style house in Bel Air, for example.

RS And there are shingle style houses in Bel Air, and they look ridiculous.

PG Have you ever had a client who asked for something that you felt was inappropriate?

RC Clients asked me to design the house in the south of France they'd always wanted, but on a site in East Hampton. It worked out very well. Since then we've had a number of clients who are Francophiles, or indeed French, who have requested French houses in East Hampton and Southampton. Although French may not be the first style to come to mind for a beach house, we stepped up to the challenge and designed what I think are very good houses that don't seem out of place.

RS We learn to love things the more we do them. We're much more comfortable with French than we used to be.

RC I can't remember another instance, though, where we were asked to do something we initially thought was inappropriate.

Top
Residence in East Hampton, New York, 2000–2004

Above
Residence on Long Island, New York, 1997–2004

PG Can a style ultimately be too successful? I remember when Bob Stern was doing the first modern shingle style houses in East Hampton more than thirty years ago, and they seemed a refreshing and welcome reconnection to a history that had been overlooked, perhaps even disdained. Thirty years later, in the age of the Farrell Building Company, a Stern house is still a rare thing, but shingle style houses are all over the place, and most of them are not very good. Is it more difficult to design a shingle style house in East Hampton today that it once was? When everyone is trying to do what you're doing, but not doing it very well, do you feel that pulls your work down, or does it allow you greater opportunity to prove what makes a RAMSA house distinctive?

RC Both. We just finished a shingle style house in Wainscott, on Georgica Pond, for discerning clients. It's very beautiful, and unique, and it doesn't look like every other shingle house you pass. So I think we are capable of stepping up the game, and even stepping up from what we ourselves did ten or twenty years ago.

RS It's unfortunate that styles do become generic. A lot of those big hedge-fund gambrel-roofed villas are visible from Route 27 on these huge spreads in the potato fields with no context. It makes you rethink what you want to do.

RC One of the houses in this book is a house in East Hampton that Peter Cook did some twenty years ago. Our clients, who built it, asked us to reimagine it for where they are in their lives today, with children and grandchildren; the wife said to make it more luxe. It wasn't a bad house, but I think we improved on it.

PG I want to go back for a minute to the question of place and regional styles. If you go back to the 1920s, which was a great decade for traditional and historicist architecture in this country, there really wasn't all that much consistency. You go to a great suburb that was built up in those years, and you'll generally find a multiplicity of styles. That in a way suggests that there's in fact historical precedent for making choices from a broader range than simply, "This is the regional style and that's what we do."

RS A lot of those suburbs were manufactured environments. Dwight James Baum had a monograph that's arranged by style, and examples of every one of those styles appear in Fieldston. There's Mediterranean, there's Tudor—it hits all the high spots. I think in suburbs you can have that mix. What ties it together is the scale and the quality of the detailing. There's a texture as you drive through the neighborhood.

PG And the landscaping and the sense of a coherent street. I think the point is that a variety of styles can contribute to a coherent streetscape in the right conditions.

RC But then we go to places like Martha's Vineyard where there truly is a regional style.

GB And sometimes we've been the architects who set the tone for a place. Roger started working on Kiawah Island in South Carolina, and he introduced the shingle style with the Beach Club and then with a house. Then I did the Ocean Course clubhouse, and after that the pattern was set: everything was shingle. Recently I started another house there and I said to the client early on, "We can do shingle, we can do low-country, or we can do a kind of European classical Schinkel-inspired house like the one I did in Seaside, Florida." For them, shingle had become the regional style, part of the appeal of the island, and so though I might have wanted to try something else equally appropriate, I'm designing a gray shingle house for them.

PG Are there particular places you feel the work of the office has had a meaningful impact?

RC East Hampton for sure. I think we've also had an influence on Martha's Vineyard.

RS We've had a very quiet impact on Martha's Vineyard, but it's been an impact. We have five houses there, and everyone knows them. They're not the biggest houses on the Vineyard, and they're not the fanciest houses on the Vineyard, but they're known for their quality and for the direction they set for subsequent development.

Top
Kiawah Island Beach Club,
Kiawah Island, South Carolina,
1992–94

Above
Ocean Course Clubhouse,
Kiawah Island, South Carolina,
2002–7

PG The Vineyard has also suffered from a lot of mediocre recent generic shingle stuff.

RS One good thing about the Vineyard is that most of the roads are lined with state forests, so you can't see most of those houses unless you fly in over them.

GB Most people don't get to see our houses either. I mean, our clients and their friends, yes; but the ordinary person doesn't see RAMSA houses except in our monographs. The way our monographs augment photos with plans hearkens back to early pattern-book houses. That's what most people see, and as Roger pointed out, it raises everybody's boat. Are these other shingle houses as literate as ours? No, but in comparison to what was being built twenty years ago, before people had any idea of building a traditional shingle house, it's an improvement.

PG   Randy said something similar when he mentioned people looking at your books. Are you flattered or troubled when you see a RAMSA house knocked off?

RS & RC   Amused!

RS   I live in New Jersey and went into a development on the former Kean estate in Livingston called Bel Air. In the middle is the old Kean house, a perfectly nice old Colonial, but the streets are lined with big house after big house after big house, on half-acre lots. Down one cul-de-sac is a very obvious version of a house we did in Toronto in 1998. It just made me say, "Wow." It's different from all the other houses because it looks like an architect did it, but at the same time it's not quite right.

RC   Grant and I have each done houses in the north suburbs of Chicago, which I think everybody knows. I think we did set a standard, a standard other people there feel they can't attain, but everybody references them. Just two doors down from the house I did, someone has very literally knocked off one of our houses and by all reports is very proud of it. He felt he had a Stern house, although we had nothing to do with it.

PG   So this is a street that has a real Stern house and a faux Stern house.

RS   At some point they cross the line and it becomes plagiarism.

PG   At what point is that?

RS   When they actually say it's a Stern house—usually when it's for sale. That's happened. Sometimes you can actually tell it's a faulty line-for-line copy since they don't have access to our working drawings.

RC   Or it's a pastiche of six of our houses.

Top
Residence at Chilmark,
Martha's Vineyard,
Massachusetts, 1979–83

Above
Residence at North York,
Toronto, Ontario, Canada,
1993–98

RS   I don't think anyone's ever gotten close enough for us to pursue them, unless they try to sell it as a Stern house.

GB   It's flattering in a way that by now our office's houses are status items. There are so many other houses to draw on, if you look at the history of traditional houses in America. But most architects aren't interested in the history of architecture, and our books are easily available, so that's where people will go instead of looking at McKim, Mead & White houses or Peabody and Stearns houses or Harrie T. Lindeberg houses.

PG   Although it's not likely that they'd knock them off any more successfully than they do yours!

GB   I would say also: big windows. People like traditional houses, but the windows on older houses are smaller than people want today, especially those with incredible ocean or mountain views.

RC   And then those earlier houses don't really have the spaces that a modern family wants. They don't have a family room, or a master suite as we conceive them today, for example, so it's easier to take one of our plans and translate it.

PG   So in a way, what you're doing with houses is the single-family house equivalent of what the firm achieved at 15 Central Park West, the condominium building that was designed with a traditional facade and massing but with larger windows to maximize views and floor plans updated for contemporary living. I once described the apartments at 15 as looking like typical Park Avenue prewar apartments that had been gut-renovated to rip out the maids' rooms and given family rooms and kitchens scaled for entertaining.

RS   Actually the apartment layouts at 15 derive from many of our house plans. The sensibility that makes our houses is where we started in this office, and it informs everything else the firm does.

PG   Are there places you especially like to work?

GM   What I think is very different about our office from many others is that we know how to work across the country. I like to work in the San Francisco area.

RS   I like to work in Los Angeles.

GM   We have work across the country, and there are very few other firms that have that broad a portfolio without having branch offices. The way it's come about is that Bob has us do the travelling. A single practitioner could never do that and have as much work as we have all over. I'm very proud of the fact that we've done work all across North America. We hug the coasts; we've done work in Chicago; we've worked in the South; and occasionally we get to work in Canada. It's fantastic that we've had that opportunity to adapt to regional sensibilities in a way that a regional architect could not or would not. And we do it very well, better than many regional architects.

RS   We're more willing to push the boundaries of what the local craftspeople and trades will do than local architects are. We come in as these brash New Yorkers, perhaps, but this is what we do and this is the level of quality we insist on, and the local trades are happy to rise to the challenge. I think we've set new standards in a lot of these areas.

PG   I think Montecito is one place that comes to mind where that's absolutely true of the work you've done.

RS   There's a pretty broad history of decently built houses there. At first glance they look very nice, well put together, but they are sort of formulaic. And actually we did Italian whereas everyone else did Spanish.

PG   A subtle but important difference. So, what characterizes a RAMSA house?

RS   They have substance.

GM   One quality people remark on is the sense of proportion in our rooms. Our houses feel comfortable—modern and livable, with lots of daylight. And the level of craftsmanship in

Top
Residence in Montecito,
Santa Barbara, California,
1993–99

Above
House on Lake Michigan,
Illinois, 2002–7

our houses is outstanding. We deliberately go out and get the best tradespeople to build our houses, and we're able to bring out the best in craftspeople wherever we work.

RC   Roger's comment about the intelligence of the planning is also key. I hear over and over from people who visit our houses that they don't feel big, even though they are, because we've come up with ways to plan houses that are not "mansion-y." That's very appealing to people who want a house the size of a mansion but don't want it to feel that way.

GB   Bob and the partners are very sophisticated in selecting house styles that feel fresh. Take Randy's house on Lake Michigan. I don't think there are many similar houses in the neighborhood. That was an entirely appropriate house style that not a lot of people had explored up to that point.

PG   What is the style of that house?

RC   I'm waiting for Gary to say.

GB   It's a big farmhouse—a picturesque rambling house that looks like it grew over time. That's a new direction that could only come from an architect with a firm grasp of history. Our houses are scholarly and knowledgeable. But if you really know the precedents, you'll see that our houses are very different—the plans, the way they're built.

PG   You might say they're idealized versions of certain traditional types?

RS   Idealized but also updated. In those older houses we look at, the bedrooms are typically upstairs; the houses are mazes of rooms; and typically they have only two, maybe three bathrooms. Fortunately, or unfortunately, in a contemporary house, the square footage required for bedrooms will outweigh what's below.

PG   How do you handle that?

Top
House at Glen Ellen,
Sonoma County, California,
2006–13

RS   Porches help. Sometimes putting the master suite on the first floor helps. Playing with the scale of the rooms downstairs helps. But it is a challenge.

GM   Another thing that differentiates our work from other offices is that our knowledge, our familiarity with and confidence in various styles, enables us to pull together ideas from different sources, making them feel fresh, which many other traditional architects practicing today don't do. They tend to be too drily academic and in the end a bit dull. We're willing to try things in ways other traditional architects are not. I just finished photographing a house in the Sonoma Valley—actually it's five buildings in a compound—and the main house, the last structure to be built, is a fusion of Bernard Maybeck, William Wurster, Schinkel, and it all came together in a way that the influences are recognizable but the whole feels different and new. I think all four of us do that quite well.

PG   That's a very important point, because if you look at the best traditional architecture from the first couple of decades of the last century, it was all very inventive. Those architects were taking vocabularies and saying new things with them. They were very rarely copying literally. The houses from the 1920s that actually mimic other buildings are rare exceptions.

Top
Brooks House,
East Hampton, New York,
1979 (unbuilt)

Center
Wiseman House,
Montauk, New York,
1965–67

Above
Residence at Chilmark,
Martha's Vineyard,
Massachusetts, 1979–83

GB I'm curious, as the newcomer: when we say "our work," when does "our work" start? Does it go back to the firm's postmodern work? If you look at our monographs, our work kept growing more and more traditional. When we send out portfolios now, we're not showing our postmodern work.

PG You've identified another point I was meaning to raise so let's deal with it right now. The firm's work has absolutely become steadily more traditional, however imaginative and inventive it may be within traditional vocabularies. So how about the postmodern approach with which the firm began, when Bob was first getting clients able to build houses important enough to notice? Is that a part of history you all acknowledge today? What is the general attitude toward all of that?

RS As the most senior in terms of tenure, I was here for the late years and then the demise of postmodernism in our practice. The first house project I worked on in the office was for Joe Brooks—*the* Joe Brooks.

PG The late Joe Brooks.

RS The late, "You Light Up My Life" Joe Brooks. It was a new take on a traditional Colonial house. The exterior had a new level of correctness and straightness to it that I don't think the office had seen until then. Bob and I were looking at English precedents much more literally than he had before.

PG I remember Bob saying he was quoting Lutyens in some of the very postmodern houses, but in fact it was a distant and strained connection.

RS Right, and with the Brooks house we were more interested in actually taking details we'd never done before and not making it a pastiche. It was a fun project; it was never built. For the same project we designed a guest house and pool house that were even more frankly a take on Homewood, a Lutyens house, in terms of massing and fenestration and everything. So we acknowledged it; it's there. But I also worked on a house in Chilmark. It was the second house I worked on, and I think of it as a transitional house insofar as again it picked up on traditional detailing more literally than we had done before, and I think that gave the house a lot more weight than our more truly postmodern houses had.

RC I remember when I was in graduate school there was an exhibit of the office's work. When I saw that house, I just loved it; I said, "That's what I want to do."

RS I visit that house every summer, for better or worse, and you know, it's still not a period piece. It's one of the first houses we did that is timeless inside, and it's not trying to be anything it's not.

PG I agree, and in some ways the house in Quogue was has some of those same qualities.

RC It was a little more cartoony. The earliest houses were tongue-in-cheek, with Bob coming out of the modernist tradition and wanting to do something more traditional, but not really feeling it was acceptable.

RS That kind of architecture works at a certain scale. About five years ago I visited the Lang house, which I'd never been to. It had become a sad, sad place. It had been painted white; it was sort of disintegrating. But the moves on it are actually witty and fun; it's a very interesting house. I just can't imagine it translating into a larger scale.

PG Bob, early in his career, was so influenced by Robert Venturi that I think, in a lot of those houses, he was trying to be Bob Venturi, and then he discovered it was better to be Bob Stern, and he gradually moved away from that. Venturi did Venturi better than Stern did, and as Bob came more fully into his own, he discovered that his voice really was traditional more than what we were calling postmodern.

RS I think one factor—maybe our clients don't want to hear this—but one factor that helped us get past that postmodern phase is that the budgets grew. Our clients were willing to spend more money to get the quality of construction that enabled us to give them the substance that makes them more timeless.

PG So do you think it's a matter of substance, a sense of heft or gravitas, that characterizes the transition from postmodern to more purely traditional?

GB We were trying to bring back all the crafts and trades that made traditional houses wonderful, and they just weren't there. It's like learning how to be a tailor. Probably the first garment you make, you might not know how to sew a sleeve on a jacket, but the more you do it and the more you study the craft of tailoring or architecture, you learn this is how a cornice is done, this is how an eave is done.

PG And that those shouldn't be reinvented.

GB It's not that it's not reinvented; it's the difference between off-the-rack and couture.

RS I think our earliest houses were a lot more self-conscious than our houses have been for the past twenty-five years. I think we are more comfortable, that we've shed our egos, so that we're making great houses that work, not great reflections of our cleverness and how much we know.

PG Bob and the firm grew, and you might argue that as he grew as an artist, and the firm grew as a business, you were changing with the times. Roger, before we started this conversation, you made an important point about the relationship between the houses and the other work in the office, and your relationship to the other partners.

RS The partners have worked together as a group for a long time. Paul Whalen, Graham Wyatt, and Alex Lamis have been here essentially as long as I have. We've been working in parallel, playing in the same sandbox, for quite a while. Our work has necessarily informed each other's by osmosis, if not by intent. We started doing apartments—that's the first thing we did— and it wasn't until we had been around for ten years or so that we did our first nonresidential building and commercial interiors and things like that. So necessarily our approach to architecture, from planning to detailing, started in residential types. Nonresidential work requires different kinds of thinking, but none of us has wanted to leave behind the attention to quality and substance that make our buildings feel like they've been there—not because they look old, but because they have a visual weight. That informs all of the firm's architecture, whether it's traditional or modernist or something in between, no matter how big it is.

Top
Lawson House,
East Quogue, New York,
1979–81

Above
Lang House,
Washington, Connecticut,
1973–74

PG Clearly there are advantages to being part of a larger enterprise. And it seems to me all four of you can say that you're influencing the direction of the firm as a whole. But that suggests another question: now that the office is so big, how much interaction is there among the partners on a daily basis?

RS There's a lot of interaction, but I think it has to be more intentional. We're on four or five floors now, so we're separated from each other physically. All of the house people don't sit in one place. We have to take it upon ourselves to see what everyone else is doing, and for them to see what we're doing.

PG Do the partners meet as a group often?

GM Yes. Weekly.

GB But not about design.

RC Funnily enough, the recession had one good effect on the partnership: we found that because there was a scarcity of work for a period that when a project would come in, more than one partner would be involved, and we've continued with that as business has gotten better; we've learned that projects can be better with more than one partner working on them. I'm working with Alex Lamis on a large office interiors project. He brings skills I don't have, but I have skills he doesn't have, and in the end it will be a better project because we're both on it.

PG How many projects are any of you likely to take on at once? How many things are on your desks at the moment?

RC Well, Grant is redesigning all of China.

GM I've been involved in fewer houses in recent years because, yes, I do work on a lot of other types of projects as well. I've been working with Paul Whalen in China, where we're doing a variety of residential work—apartment building complexes and whole neighborhoods, in addition to some single-family houses. But to answer your question, I probably have about a dozen, maybe fifteen quite large-scale projects, at present.

GB It's not just the four of us—each of us has our own team.

PG Do your teams work only for you? Do you share junior architects? Do they move back and forth between projects?

RS The office has a studio system. Each of us is a studio head, and there are three others. The people in the studios are working on the projects we have. If I have seven projects, the fifteen or so people I have in my studio are working on those projects. We're about to make a concerted effort to move people from studio to studio for their own good, and for ours as well.

PG So there's a certain amount of rotation among the studios?

RS Not enough. But we're trying. It's hard because everyone wants to see a project through, and it takes a long time to build a building.

RC   But each of us has a number of more senior people who are maybe forty years old and have been with the firm for ten or fifteen years who are in our studios and on whom we depend.

PG   So in some ways each studio is almost a firm within the firm, but with the assets of the whole firm.

RS   Yes, that's correct.

GM   And going back to one of the first things we discussed, which is why we stayed with the firm, we have our independence, but we have the advantages of a larger office that we can draw on.

PG   Right. Clearly you'd be very unlikely to be doing the work you're doing in China if you were off on your own.

GM   Yes, that's right.

GB   And to some extent we do work together. We've done so many houses in the past thirty years, and really exceptional houses, that although I'm not constantly talking to Roger about why he did this or that, all of his drawings and photos and precedents are available to each of us and so we can say, "Oh! That's how Roger solved this challenge in this plan." So though we may not talk about it directly, we still have a creative synergy. It's still a kind of conversation.

PG   How much effort is there to not repeat yourselves?

RC   A lot.

PG   While you've done many shingle style houses, and many Georgian houses, and so forth, I can't think of any two Stern houses that really look exactly like each other.

RC   There are occasions when people come to us and say, "I want that house."

PG   What do you say in those moments?

RC   I've learned to say okay because I know the house will end up different. Even when clients say that, they'll have their own program, or their site is different. There are so many variables. I know their house is going to end up unique from the one that brought them to us.

RS   And often it's not what is in the photographs that they want. What they want is the feeling they get from the photographs.

PG   So what you're saying is that ultimately you can capture that feeling but in a different context. So you start with telling them you can do the house they come in saying they want because you know it will evolve into something else.

RC   Right, and so we never say, "Oh no, we won't do that again."

PG   You're all established enough that some clients come to you directly, and you certainly have repeat clients. But in the case of new clients who know the firm but don't know you as distinct from one another, how is it determined which partner they actually end up with?

GB Sometimes it's by region. If Grant has done work in Sonoma or San Francisco, it makes sense for him to continue working in that region. Sometimes when a prospective client says they like a particular house we've done, it makes sense to match them with the partner who designed it.

RS If not, then we discuss it as a group, and between us we choose what fits. We try to get a sense of what the chemistry is. There are people who have connections to Bob and call him directly, and then through the course of the conversation, he'll decide which of us is best to work with them.

GB I would say, too, that Roger and Randy have done a lot of the big estate houses, and the houses I work on are small-lot houses. The decisions are also based on our experience with house types.

PG That makes very logical sense.

RC Our East Hampton clientele has been a huge source of work for me, both houses and apartments.

PG We know that Randy owns East Hampton.

RC A couple of years ago a woman called and said, "I'm so-and-so, and it seemed inevitable that I would call you." And she hired us.

PG Could you each talk for a moment about a couple of the houses you're associated with that you consider particularly meaningful to you, or that you're especially proud of, or that are significant in any other way—perhaps even a house that for some reason you're unhappy about.

RC Roger, you're first.

RS One of the most interesting houses I worked on that's in this book is one in Malibu, and what's most distinctive about it is that it's actually five or six different buildings that work together as a true compound. That's partially because the sites were assembled sequentially and houses were built on them, but our clients had made a conscious decision to break up the scale of a pretty complex program by creating a kind of village. It was really quite challenging: the site is a hillside on a bluff, with strict height limitations; we had to do buildings that conformed to very stringent codes and pull it off as architecture at the same time. And we had to do it without appearing self-conscious about it, without putting our egos into it. It's as much a reflection of our clients' aspirations as it is about what we wanted it to be.

Top
Encinal Bluffs Family Compound,
Malibu, California,
1995–2007

Above
Residence in Pacific Heights,
San Francisco, California,
1994–99

PG That's actually the second time the word "self-conscious" has come into the conversation. At the end of the day I think that's really the most important distinction between the post-modern work and your current work. The postmodern work was highly self-conscious, and often quite mannered, whereas the current work almost always seems un-self-conscious.

RS I think that's also the distinction between us and other architects practicing today, even in the traditional mode. I don't think our clients have the sense that their houses were foisted on them by us. I think they see it as a collaborative process.

GM For me, one of the most gratifying experiences I've had is with a couple from San Francisco. I designed their house in San Francisco back in 1994. We did an apartment here in New York, in the Chatham, a few floors above Bob's apartment. And then over the last decade or so I've designed five buildings for them on a property in Glen Ellen, in the Sonoma Valley. I have a great rapport with them and we know each other very well. There was a continual design dialogue as we proceeded from one project to the next. And so there's a consistency as you move from the first house to the most recent in terms of the proportions of the rooms as well as some of the detailing; everything feels familiar and everything is comfortable for them. It's just been a wonderful experience for me in that they've come back and allowed me to explore possibilities with them, whether it's a house in the city or in a beautiful countryside setting. The Glen Ellen property has a range of structures: two on top of a hill and three in the valley. One site is exposed to 270-degree views and the other is quite intimate, so between them they offer two completely different effects. I treasure the experience of having known them and worked with them over many years—nearly twenty years. It's been fantastic.

PG It's must be great to have a client who feels you understand their needs and their sensibilities well enough that they don't have to go through the whole rigmarole of explaining what they are.

RC It's an important point: each of us has a number of clients with whom we have twenty- or thirty-year relationships.

GM Often at first meeting we tell them we're going to know more about them at the end of the project than they'd ever wished us to know. It's just the reality.

PG Which is why chemistry is so important.

GM There's a high level of trust.

GB I did a house in Seaside, Florida, which is a bit of an architects' playground. This was our clients' third house there; this house is just behind the dune. There are codes in Seaside that mean each house on the water is essentially a box; that was a given, and the height was a given, and the slope of the roof was a given, and I told Andrés Duany, who wrote the guidelines, that all we got to do was decide where to put the windows! But Seaside is relatively free of regional stylistic expectations so I was able to do a house based on European precedents like Schinkel, Alexander "Greek" Thomson, and Plečnic; we could get away with that there. There was a bit more architectural freedom.

PG Right, because the code is not stylistically prescriptive.

GB The first houses at Seaside were built on a shoestring, like our early postmodern houses, but by the time I got there, Seaside was a big success, and people were willing to spend more, and it's a lot more fun to build a house with a bigger budget.

PG I would think so. Randy, is there a project you'd like to discuss?

RC Two actually, at two extremes in terms of scale and budget. One is a house on Buzzards Bay, a big shingle-style house where we were given no restraints. It's at the end of a 2.5 mile long peninsula, so it feels like it's at the end of the earth. This particular client had a house there with his first wife, and he had a new wife who wanted a new house, and so I was encouraged to

Top
House at Apaquoque,
East Hampton, New York,
1989–93

Above
Seaside Cottage,
Seaside, Florida,
2001–6

do whatever I wanted to do. I was able to draw in craftsmen I'd worked with to do specialty details throughout the house, which was a lot of fun. When you're given no restraints, it's almost harder because you have only yourself holding you back. It was a remarkable project. Then on the other end of the spectrum is a renovation I did for Ken Lipper, where we took the house of the artist Claus Hoie, which Ken didn't want to tear down; it was just kind of a nothing, one-story house, but he wanted to keep the spirit of the previous owners.

PG   That's on Hook Pond in East Hampton, right?

RC   Yes, on Hook Pond Lane. To preserve the spirit and also to perk up the house and make something of it. We didn't have a big budget, but it was a fun project and Ken was a great client to work with. And it was an opportunity to add a modern element, which is not something I'm often called upon to do.

Top
House on Buzzards Bay,
South Dartmouth,
Massachusetts, 2003–7

PG   Let's conclude by coming back to the process of design and how it works, how it is or isn't different from that of other firms. I don't want you just to tell me that the design process at RAMSA is better. What makes it what it is?

RC   What we hear over and over again as we go different places is that other house architects use our books for inspiration, whereas our frame of reference is McKim, Mead & White or Harrie T. Lindeberg or Carrère & Hastings. We start with primary sources when we design our houses.

PG   We know it's not an accident that the first room one enters in this office is the library. That has enormous symbolic impact, but when I'm here I'm always struck by the fact that it's not just there for show. You see people scanning the shelves and taking and returning stacks of books. So I presume that using the library is part of the work of all of you.

RC   And what you see in the library is only the tip of the iceberg of our collection today.

GB   Another difference is our model-building process. When we start on a house, we don't just draw up plans, especially for houses that want to be rambling or picturesque; we build little clay study models at the same time. We're looking at the plan and the model, and then at the model and the plan, how the rooflines work—hardly anyone else talks about that any more. When you show a client or a contractor or an interior designer something in three dimensions, it's easier for them to understand it. People who know their property and know how they want to live are able to contribute unexpected ideas with this more interactive process. Then we go from clay models to bigger paper and foamcore models, and when the house is finished, we hear: "Oh! it looks just like the model!" And that's a good thing because there are no surprises; all the kinks were worked out in small scale with inexpensive materials.

RC   At our very first meeting with a new client, we show a complete concept with a model, renderings, floor plans that are furnished, a site plan that suggests a direction for the landscape. It's the whole picture. As I understand it, many other architects start with just a floor plan and then end up in a bad place, which is often when clients come to us.

PG   It's true that RAMSA doesn't give you rooms you can't figure out how to furnish. Clearly that is always well thought out.

RS From the very beginning.

RC Each of us is interested in interior design and landscape design. We look at a house holistically. If someone says, "Where should we put the swimming pool?" we don't tell them they need to go to a landscape architect. Or "Where should we put the sofa?" we don't send them to a decorator.

PG The firm often does interior design in-house, right?

RS We have an interior design group, but many of our residential clients come to us with an interior designer.

GM If there's one thing I've noticed with our house clients, it's at our initial meeting when we've talked about the architecture, the interiors, the landscape, and everything, and as we wrap up, they say, "You've got it! You've answered all our questions. You know how the house is to be furnished; you know how we live; how we relate the inside to the outside," and so on. And they are usually surprised at how quickly we can come to a solution that summarizes their lifestyle and captures their expectations of what they want in their house. That's very gratifying. It's rare that we have to start again and redo the concept. With Roger and a house he's designing now, after the first meeting, the clients said, "Just build it! We're done!"

RS Yes, but of course that house has been evolving since then. Without sounding too Kumbaya-ish, I think we've struck a balance between doing the architecture we want to do and incorporating what our clients want into that architecture. I don't think any of us—Bob Stern included—come across as prima donnas. A lot of prospective clients are afraid of that when they first come in. They see the big name on the door and think, "You're going to tell me what to do and how to live." But we're not interested in doing that, and our clients appreciate it.

HOUSE ON LAKE MICHIGAN

There's a certain ease to be found in the communities along Lake Michigan, a quality that prevails in this North Shore village, about twenty miles from Chicago. You see as many Arts and Crafts–style bungalows as grand homes, and there is a distinctly Midwestern, all-American flavor to the place. Most of the original lakefront estates have been broken up into more modest properties, but our clients were fortunate enough to find one that remained intact. On the three-acre site, the suburban flavor of the street frontage gives way to a more countrified experience at the property's mid-section, before falling away to a crescent-shaped stretch of beach.

A 1920s Colonial Revival house had occupied the site, and the style is prevalent in the area. Our clients, a couple with three children, had something very different in mind. They talked to us about an American Georgian farmhouse of the sort seen typically in New England, built from fieldstone, clapboard, and white-painted brick—a vision inspired less by style preferences than the desire for a welcoming, family-oriented way of life.

25

SITE PLAN

0 10 20   40 ft

While we embraced this idea, turning it into architecture proved to be challenging. Our clients' requirements added up to a substantial program, which translated into a large house. Yet they were, paradoxically, adamant about not wanting the place to look big. Or to feel that way, either. The rooms were to be modestly sized—the word "cozy" was invoked frequently. There were also constraints related to the property's abundance of massive old trees. The husband (to his credit) wouldn't allow the removal of a single one, requiring that we maneuver the structure into the setting.

The couple's material preferences helped us to break up the building, so that it seemed more episodic and, consequently, less monolithic. We finished the center portion in the white-painted brick typically associated with the Georgian style; the wings at either end were built from fieldstone; clapboard above the garages on the front facade and the second floor of a volume in the rear suggests more informal secondary spaces. We also used a porte-cochere to, in effect, divide the front elevation in two, by placing it perpendicular to the approximate midpoint of the facade. When you arrive in the motor court, the projecting stone volume screens off half the house. And we kept the structure light on its feet with a narrow footprint that introduced multiple courtyards. In addition to facilitating a design rich in vignettes, this gambit brought abundant southern and western light into the house, to augment the morning sun coming across the lake from the east.

Above
Our design was influenced by David Adler's 1928 William McCormick Blair house in Lake Bluff, a Colonial Georgian-style farmhouse combining a central block and a rambling composition of gabled wings clad in white-painted clapboard and fieldstone.

Similarly, we used the plan to make the structure seem smaller from within. In the firm's residential projects, we often create a visual axis through the major rooms, which makes even a big house feel legible; here, we added two cross-axes that suggest a comfortable parity between the residence's formal public spaces and those casual areas in which contemporary families spend most of their time.

Entering through the front door, one is greeted by a view straight through the entry hall and out across the lawn to the lake. From that point, you can proceed to the right, into the living room and adjoining library or up the double-height main stair hall that leads directly to the master suite; turning left, you move down the hall toward the dining room, a big kitchen/breakfast space, and the family room. More often than not, however, the family comes into the house from the porte-cochere or the motor court just beyond it. This secondary entrance is just as effective as the primary one: the door that opens from the porte-cochere looks straight through the house, presenting a sight line through the mudroom and a short service corridor across the kitchen's breakfast table and out to the view. This procession also passes a back stair, which leads up to the children's bedrooms, giving parents and kids separate ways of accessing their private areas.

The rooms on both the formal and casual sides intercommunicate: we created an enfilade of openings from the dining room through the center hall to the living room and, beyond it, the library. There is a broad pocket door between the kitchen/breakfast area and the family room. Even though the residence's self-contained sides stand in a balanced counterpoint, they're not isolated from one another: a long axial gallery becomes a natural passage from end to end.

Although the rooms, in keeping with the clients' wishes, are smaller than one would expect to find in a structure of this scale, most are articulated by muscular interior architecture: mouldings, paneling, door surrounds, wainscoting, pilasters, and beams, and the vocabulary is simpler or more elaborate depending upon a room's function and character. The grandest is the library, which is strongly detailed and finished in oak. The couple's desire for a human-scaled residence,

moreover, gave rise to a series of moments that contributed to the gracious domestic narrative. The bay window in the kitchen, for example, is a nook with doors on either side overlooking a covered porch, an enveloping zone for a two-person chat. The butler's pantry evolved into a multipurpose room with glass-fronted cabinets for displaying china, a sink and counter suitable for flower arranging, and space to lay a buffet for a casual dinner. And the wife's request for a quiet spot suitable for talking with her two young girls became a seat below the large Palladian window at the landing of the main stair.

This project involved a lot of back and forth with both of our clients, having to do less with form-making than finding our way to the essential character of the house. Ultimately we succeeded in achieving their goal of a large house that feels, not like a mansion, but a home.

Randy Correll, Project Partner

Opposite

The projecting volumes of
the rear facade, which give the
house a picturesque quality,
shape a series of outdoor living
spaces that face the lake.

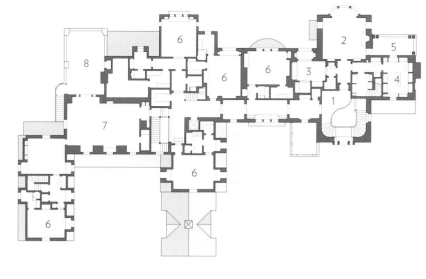

KEY TO FIRST FLOOR
1. ENTRY HALL
2. MAIN STAIR
3. LIVING ROOM
4. LIBRARY
5. GALLERY
6. DINING ROOM
7. BUTLER'S PANTRY
8. KITCHEN
9. FAMILY ROOM
10. SCREENED PORCH
11. FAMILY STAIR
12. OFFICE
13. MUDROOM
14. GARAGE

KEY TO SECOND FLOOR
1. UPPER STAIR HALL
2. MASTER BEDROOM
3. MASTER BATH
4. DRESSING ROOM
5. PORCH
6. BEDROOM
7. EXERCISE ROOM
8. TERRACE

SECOND FLOOR PLAN

0   10   20   40 ft

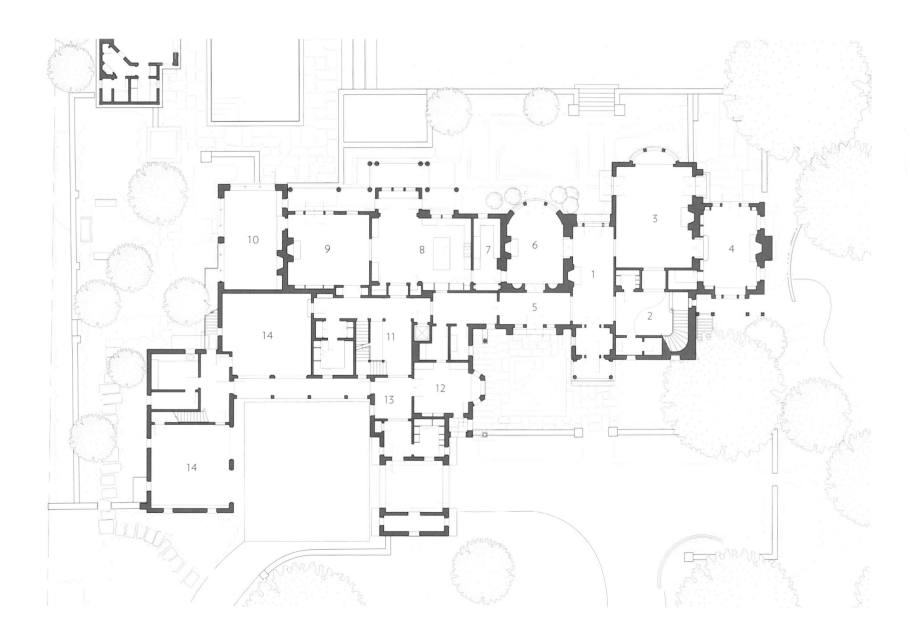

FIRST FLOOR PLAN

0   5   10   20 ft

Below, left
The entry garden, composed
of clipped boxwood parterres,
is framed by the front porch
and the north wing. A projecting
pergola shades the bay window and extends the garden
experience.

Below
Massive stone chimneys, a
projecting porch, and a two-story
bay add volumetric interest
and surface animation to the
facade at the south end of
the house.

Overleaf
An informal flower garden,
created by landscape
architect Douglas Hoerr,
provides a shaded oasis
off the screened porch.

Below
With its fireplace, enticing lake
views, and glimpses into the
major public rooms, the entry
hall is a welcoming space.

Below, left

The entry vestibule offers a buffer between the sometimes frigid winter air and the entry hall. A leaded-glass transom and side lights surround the French doors and mirror the design for the entry door.

Below, right

The dining room is scaled for smaller functions and family gatherings rather than grand affairs. French doors leading to the main gallery are flanked by Georgian-inspired shell-top cabinets.

Left
The library, off the living room, is paneled in English oak with a strongly carved frieze and fireplace mantel.

Left, below
A semi-elliptical bay window in the living room offers sweeping lake views. As the family proposed, the room is scaled to accommodate a single intimate seating area. The French doors open onto a garden shared with the adjoining library.

Right

The breakfast area of the kitchen is open to the family room, but it can be closed off with pocketing glazed doors, which mute noise but maintain a visual connection.

Below, left

In its details, the paneling in the family room draws on an Arts and Crafts vocabulary and is simpler than in the house's formal rooms. The doorway to the right of the fireplace leads to the screened porch.

Below, right

An alcove off the kitchen, flanked by doors and with a lake view, is a cozy place for informal chats.

Opposite

The kitchen is designed for casual meals and conversation as well as cooking. The coffered ceiling adds texture and interest, and elegantly nests the recessed lighting.

Opposite, below

The butler's pantry, which is used as a buffet serving area, features lighted china cabinets with leaded-glass windows and mahogany countertops.

Below

The gallery connecting the house's formal and informal ends draws in south light from the entry garden.

Left and opposite
A window seat, within a deeply
recessed Palladian window
on a landing of the main stair,
provides both a physical and
visual pause between floors.

Left, below
The upstairs hallway leading to
the children's rooms includes
a window seat flanked by a pair
of homework desks.

Below, right

For the mirror-paneled master bath, which captures and reflects the abundant light and views, we created a mosaic floor in concert with interior designer Victoria Hagan.

Bottom, right

The wife's dressing room, paneled in bleached oak, is detailed to evoke the feminine elegance of the 1920s.

Bottom, left

A built-in desk and bookshelves in one of the children's rooms create a sense of self-containment. The window seat is sized for an occasional sleepover.

Below
Distressed oak paneling lines
the billiards room; the elevated
banquettes enable the players
to keep an eye on the game
while relaxing.

Opposite
The temperature-controlled
wine storage space connects via
glazed doors to a handsomely
appointed tasting room where
dessert is often served.

Below
The pool and terrace center on
the screened porch; the terrace
above communicates with the
exercise room and provides a
platform for yoga with a view.

From the screened porch the view extends over the pool to the lake through a stand of mature trees.

Below
The screens in the porch can be exchanged for glass in the cold months. Painted horizontal boards, a robust granite mantelshelf, and a reclaimed-brick floor reinforce the outdoor character.

Below, left
The pathway leading down from the pool area arrives at a sun deck atop the boathouse before reaching the beach. Douglas Hoerr selected native plantings to give the bank a natural appearance.

Below, right
The terrace off the library is an intimate outdoor gathering place.

RESIDENCE ON BEL AIR ROAD

Comprising four acres in Los Angeles at the foot of a hillside district and within hailing distance of several examples of Wallace Neff's Mediterranean architecture, the site for this house was developed by Paul Williams in the 1960s for a Regency Revival villa. That structure was demolished before our clients purchased the property and, notwithstanding the site's history and surroundings, they asked us to design a house inspired by the stone and slate architecture of the East Coast. On visits to their children at college in Philadelphia, the couple had fallen in love with the early twentieth-century Norman French estates of that city's suburbs, particularly Chestnut Hill. Given Robert Stern's definitive study of the architecture of George Howe—whose firm was responsible for much of what they admired—we were happy to oblige.

Freely adapting the parti of Mellor, Meigs and Howe's Francis S. McIlhenny house (1918), we organized our design around a sequence of courtyards and garden rooms, each of the latter focused about a principal facade. As each elevation with its

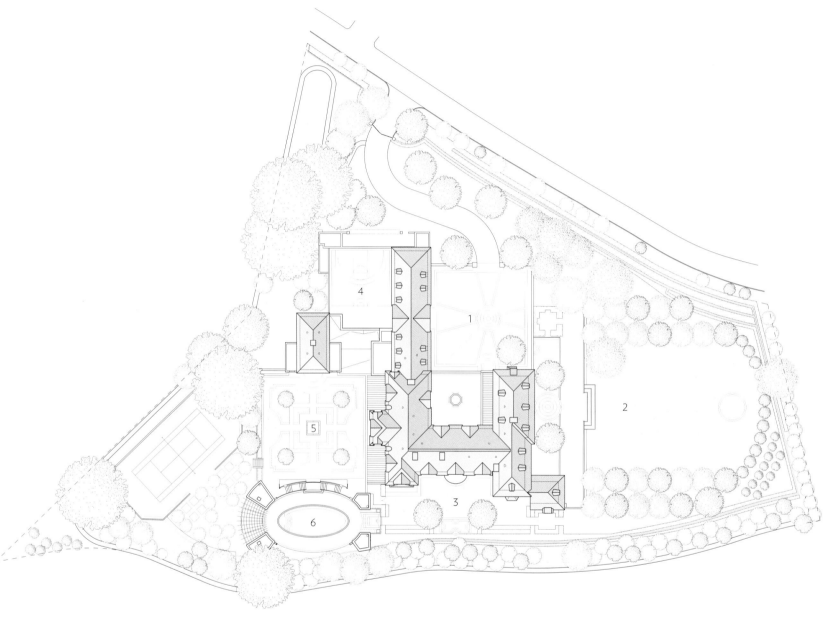

Opposite

Our precedents included
Norman French chateaux and
early-twentieth-century
Norman revival houses in the
United States, specifically
Mellor, Meigs and Howe's
McIlhenny house in Chestnut
Hill, Pennsylvania.

KEY TO SITE PLAN
1. MOTOR COURT
2. MAIN LAWN
3. KOI GARDEN
4. SERVICE COURT
5. ROSE PARTERRE
6. POOL

SITE PLAN

0   15   30   60 ft

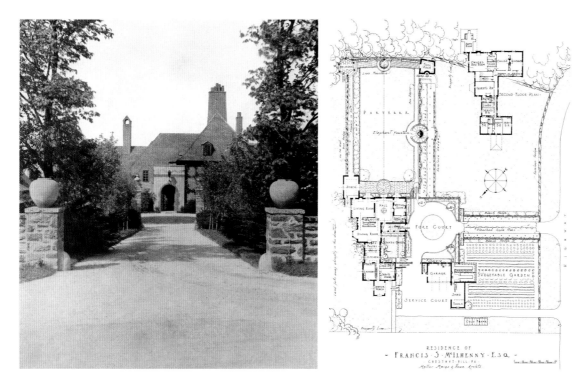

RESIDENCE OF
- FRANCIS · J · McILHENNY · ESQ -
CHESTNUT · HILL · PA ·

adjacent garden has a distinctive character of its own, the full extent of what is in fact a substantial structure is not immediately apparent from any one point on the ground, and the house achieves an intimacy of scale despite its true size. The garden walls and clipped plantings extending from the facades reinforce this effect, as they extend the architecture into the landscape and screen the rest of the house from view.

From the motor court, one enters the house through tall arched wooden doors into a loggia along one side of a cloister-like fountain courtyard. At forty-four feet square, this entry court allows ample sunlight into the loggia and interior galleries along two of its other sides, which in turn link the principal rooms that are set against the garden facades. To the east, the living room, entry hall, and library are arranged enfilade and open to the main terrace and lawn beyond. On the south side, a broad gallery extends from the entry hall and passes the main stair and dining room, which overlook a smaller garden centered on an elaborate koi fountain. The gallery ends in the family room, flanked by twin pergolas shading the breakfast room and den and framing a rose parterre. Behind this last group of rooms runs the family hall, passing along the third side of the entry court to connect with the service entry, porte cochere, and garage beyond.

As on the main floor, the circulation spaces on the upper level look onto the entry court so that bedrooms have the maximum amount of privacy as well as the preferred garden views. The area above the formal living areas is given to the master suite, consisting of his-and-her baths and dressing rooms and a sitting room in addition to the bedroom itself. The remainder of this floor, facing south and west, contains the children's and guest suites along with staff quarters.

A separate wing, physically attached to the main house but entered independently, contains the gym and a sitting room at grade with guest quarters above. It forms the northern edge of the rose parterre and sits opposite the overlook to an elliptical swimming pool and surrounding terrace.

In detailing this project we followed our precedents by relying on materials, craftsmanship, and color to provide scale, character, and warmth. On the exterior, we took care to emphasize hand work, from the skillfully cut and laid up rubble Ontario limestone of the walls, to the rough-hewn timber porch columns and lintels, to the finely wrought iron railings and gates. Employing an

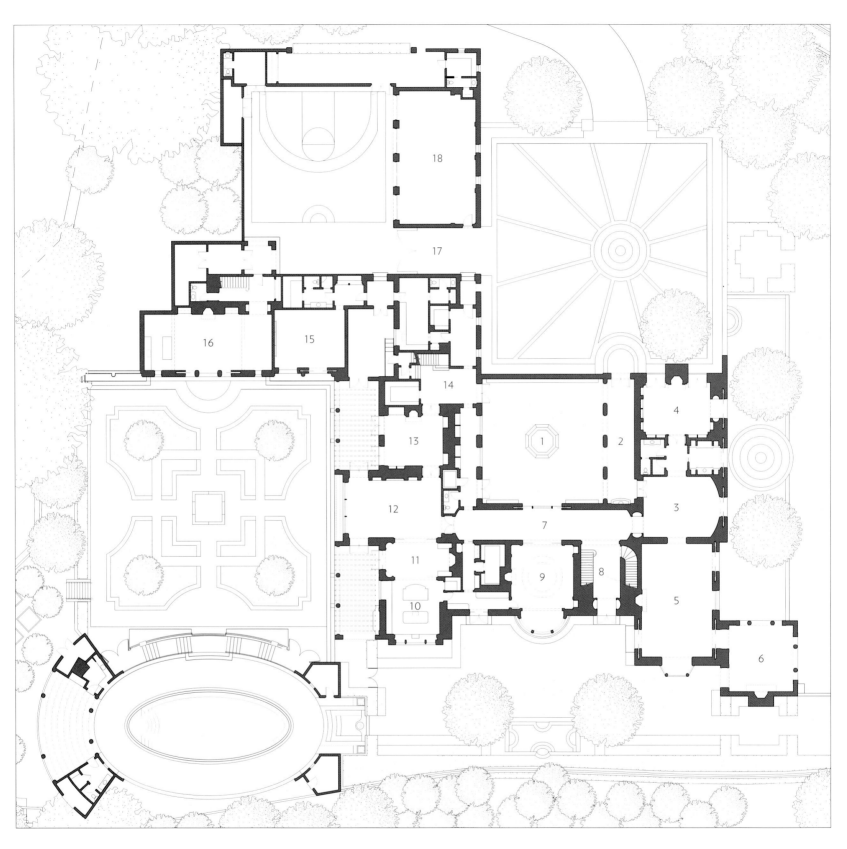

KEY TO FIRST FLOOR
1. ENTRY COURT
2. LOGGIA
3. ENTRY HALL
4. LIBRARY
5. LIVING ROOM
6. COVERED PORCH
7. GALLERY
8. MAIN STAIR
9. DINING ROOM
10. KITCHEN
11. BREAKFAST ROOM
12. FAMILY ROOM
13. DEN
14. FAMILY STAIR
15. GYM
16. GUEST HOUSE
    LIVING ROOM
17. PORTE COCHERE
18. GARAGE

KEY TO SECOND FLOOR
1. SITTING ROOM
2. MASTER BEDROOM
3. MASTER SITTING ROOM
4. HER BATH
5. HER DRESSING ROOM
6. HIS BATH
7. HIS DRESSING ROOM
8. BEDROOM
9. STAFF
10. GUEST HOUSE BEDROOM

FIRST FLOOR PLAN

0   15   30 ft

SECOND FLOOR PLAN

0   15   30   60 ft

old carpenter's trick, the rough-cut roofing slates decrease in thickness and exposure as they rise up each slope, making the roof seem taller and steeper. Hand-made brick details around the doors and windows, along the eaves, and inserted as string coursing between floors add a smaller scale and earthy tone to the main body of the house. Rose-toned stucco on the garage wing, guest house, and living room porch further soften the impression of bulk and mass.

The restrained but refined interior evokes the modern classicism that was more or less contemporaneous with the precedents we studied for the plan and exterior detailing. The suppressed casings and simplified cove moulding of the entry hall, for example, and streamlined Georgian details of the crotch-mahogany library draw on French *moderne* as well as Hollywood Regency. Interior ironwork, such as the main stair railing, is inspired equally by the modernism of Edgar Brandt and Fritz Kühn and the traditionalism of Samuel Yellin. In the public rooms, our details, combined with the fourteen-foot ceilings and deep, articulated openings between adjacent spaces, give the architecture a robustness to balance that of the exterior. In more private areas such as the master bedroom, the smaller spaces and lower ceilings favor a more intimate and literal vocabulary of French paneled rooms en suite.

Although its sources lie in different regions and periods, this project was conceived with our clients' lifestyle—and the southern California climate—in mind. The house and its site were envisioned as a stage for large-scale entertaining. Throughout the main level, the paired exterior doors and their screens recess fully into walls, virtually transforming the rooms into loggias and maximizing an easy flow between indoors and out. Covered porches and pergolas provide shaded buffers from the sun, as do the allées of sycamores and groves of fruit trees further out in the landscape. Water—traditionally a key player in California architecture—flows in fountains and pools in each of the gardens as a cooling element and soothing backdrop.

At the same time this remains, and functions exceptionally well as, a family home. The interior is organized into discrete, manageable suites of rooms tied together by circulation and clear sightlines; the exterior and its landscape are experienced—and perceived—incrementally so as not to be overpowering. The house sustains its residential and anecdotal character within an undeniably grand context, and it achieves a carefully modulated balance between the two.

Roger Seifter, Project Partner

Above
An aerial view shows the house organized around an internal courtyard, with each of the principal facades opening onto an outdoor "room" that is clearly defined with plantings and hardscape.

Overleaf
A sycamore-lined gravel drive opens onto the square motor court, bounded on three sides by high stone garden walls and the imposing end of the main block of the house. On the fourth side the lowered eave and rose-colored stucco facing of the service wing establish a hierarchy of scale and materials.

Below

Since each wing of the house
opens onto or overlooks the
entry court, this cloister-like space
is its formal and symbolic heart.
On warm evenings the splash
from the center fountain can
be heard throughout the house.

Opposite, above

The facade overlooking the
main lawn is the most imposing
elevation. French doors pocket
fully into the walls, virtually
transforming the rooms behind
them into covered porches.

Opposite, below

A covered porch off the living
room is aligned with one of
the sycamore allées that frame
the main lawn. Stucco walls,
an antique terra-cotta floor, and
a stained fir ceiling establish
the space—as tall as it is wide—
as a shaded transition between
indoors and out.

Right and below

Water features such as this
koi fountain are focal points
in the landscape that extend
the visual axes inside the
house. Here the curves of the
pool walls echo the rounded
bay of the dining room directly
across the garden.

Opposite, above

In the evening the lights shining through the oversized doors and windows show the degree of openness and porosity that the masonry architecture achieves.

Opposite, below

The family end of the main house and the guest house overlook a rose parterre, the most formal of the gardens.

Below

The elliptical pool is set a half-story below the rose parterre. Its shape echoes the curves of the surrounding walls, steps, and pavilions. Wood lattice covers the structures around the pool, providing a leghold for plantings that soften and meld them with the landscape.

Below
Stuc Pierre coursing on the walls of
the entry reinforces its function
as an intermediary space between
indoors and out. Restrained cove
mouldings and suppressed casings
emphasize the high ceiling and
thick walls.

Opposite, below
An enfilade of arched openings
extends from the living room
through the entry hall to the library.

Right

French-polished crotch mahogany paneling and pared-down classical mouldings give the library an air of streamlined modernity, juxtaposed with a Georgian chimneypiece found in London.

Right, below

A vaulted and paneled ceiling brings scale and visual interest to the living room. The room has exposures to the outside on three sides including the rounded piano bay at its far end, which overlooks the koi fountain garden.

Opposite

Particular attention was paid to the design and craftsmanship of ironwork throughout the house. The work of Harrie T. Lindeberg inspired the main stair balustrade, while the exterior railings (seen through the landing window) recall designs of the 1920s by the German blacksmith Fritz Kühn.

Right

A broad and high-ceilinged gallery, set between the more formal rooms and the kitchen/family room, can become a setting for large-scale events.

Right, below

Square dining rooms are exceptionally versatile. This room is 26 by 26 feet and accommodates a single large table or up to five smaller ones, each with seating for eight.

Below and opposite
Daily life focuses on an open kitchen/family room at the west end of the main floor. At the center is the breakfast space, with French doors to the garden on one side and a tiled inglenook fireplace on the other. Broad windows flood the kitchen with south and west light. Along with the breakfast room, it can be closed off from the family room by wide pocketing doors.

Opposite
The family room and den are informal counterpoints to the living room and library at the opposite end of the main floor. A wall of nine-foot-high windows in the family room with a sweeping view of the rose parterre transforms the space into a bright and airy garden room. The pine-paneled den, by contrast, is a secluded refuge shaded from the afternoon sun by a deep trellised porch.

Below
Nearly hidden away in the lower level and reached by its own winding stairway, the theater is one component of an entertaining suite that includes a wine cellar and billiards room as well.

Opposite
Inspired by the library at
Malmaison, her master dressing
room is configured as a three-
part suite articulated by column-
iated walls and alternating barrel-
and groin-vaulted ceilings.

Below, left and right
The elliptical bedroom and an
adjacent sitting room anchor
the master suite, an enfilade of
rooms that share a vocabulary
of French-paneled walls and
deeply coved ceilings. The
sequence culminates in her bath
and office, combined in one
luxurious space.

Bottom
A second-floor sitting room
at the top of the main stair
separates the master suite from
the children's bedrooms.

Below
The relationship between the outdoor spaces is evident in the rose parterre, whose size and proportions match those of the motor court diagonally across the site. The guest house terminates one axis of the garden.

Opposite
View from the guest house over the rose parterre to the sunken swimming-pool court.

Opposite, below
The deliberately simple and more abstract detailing in the guest house complements its contemporary furnishings. The ground floor incorporates a combined living/dining room with an open kitchen.

RESIDENCE IN HIGHLAND PARK

Our clients came to us with a wedge-shape lot overlooking a wooded ravine in a suburb not far from where they had lived for nearly thirty years. At our first interview, they expressed a preference for a shingle style residence with formal symmetry facing the street and picturesque massing facing a wooded ravine to the north and west. This was key to the development of what is in the end a very playful design. Also fundamental to the parti was the desire to provide a setting for their art collection, which had outgrown the wall space in their previous home. They were eager to take the opportunity to design a house that would support a narrative reorganization of their holdings, creating tailored settings for the artists. Designers Arlene Semel and Brian Snow were instrumental in developing the interiors to complement the art.

Working with landscape architect Douglas Hoerr of the Chicago firm Hoerr Schaudt, we created an S-shaped drive that meets the street at the southwest corner of the property and then skirts a broad lawn to arrive at a motor court on the east side of the house. The street facade, with its strong central gable, gives the impression of a small cottage. As the drive curves into the motor court, where the double-bow gable of the entrance facade is flanked to the north by the double gable of the garage and service area, visitors begin to sense the true size of the house. But it's only when one crosses the porch that casts the front door into shadow and the low entry hall that one discovers the double-height stair hall, which rises dramatically to the glazed cupola that bathes it in soft natural light. This unexpected jump in apparent scale continues into the living room, which also rises to the full height of the house with a bow-shaped ceiling and a large south-facing window that looks back across the front lawn. The library, the dining room, and the axial gallery face the woods to the west.

SITE PLAN

0 10 20   40 ft

The fulcrum between the formal entertaining rooms and the more relaxed family wing is the kitchen, where an expansive bay window embraces the ravine view. The kitchen serves both the dining room and, one step down, the family room, which, with its board-and-beam ceiling and stripped-down details, suggests the more casual nature of the space, which opens in turn to a bluestone-paved porch that overlooks the pool below.

As the sloped garden on the west side of the property tumbles down a full story to the north, the plan of the house kinks to form a loosely crescent-shaped two-story garden facade facing the wooded vista. We developed a lower-level garden platform, discrete from the more formal parts of the house, and fitted it out with a cabana, pool, and play area. Doug Hoerr's reconfiguration of the landscape opened the basement level to day-light, which enabled us to fulfill the couple's desire to provide activity space for their grandchildren with a rumpus room into which we set a large arched window flanked by two small elliptical windows to create a playfully anthropomorphic "face."

The second-floor rooms repeat the hierarchy established on the first floor, with the master suite, media room, and private study over the formal rooms and three bed-and-bath suites for guests and grandchildren over the family room, porch. The master bedroom, with its elegantly sculpted handkerchief-vault ceiling and graceful bow window oriented toward the ravine, is centered over the heart of the house.

For all the planning involved, architecture remains an inexact art; as with any creative endeavor, it represents an ongoing process of discovery. The house is as well suited to informal living—it's proven to be a grandchild magnet—as it is for our clients' frequent large philanthropic gatherings. And the expressive flexibility of the shingle style allows us to play with expectations. One of our clients' great pleasures is the reaction the place engenders when visitors first encounter the soaring stair hall: just as we predicted, they exclaim, "Oh my—what a delightful surprise!"

Grant Marani, Project Partner

Above
The pool elevation related to New Place, Haselemare, Surrrey, designed by C. F. A. Voysey in 1897.

Opposite

The entrance elevation was influenced by John Russell Pope's beautiful and playful composition at Tenacre, built for Joseph Palmer Knapp in Southampton, New York, in the 1920s. Our symmetrical interpretation shifted the entrance to the center of the facade and extended the porch from end to end.

Overleaf

The bow window enclosing the breakfast area of the kitchen and the family room and porch beyond overlook the ravine. Landscape architect Douglas Hoerr created a lush, casually planted path that meanders past the family room and porch down to the lawn adjacent to the pool.

SECOND FLOOR PLAN

0 8 16 32 ft

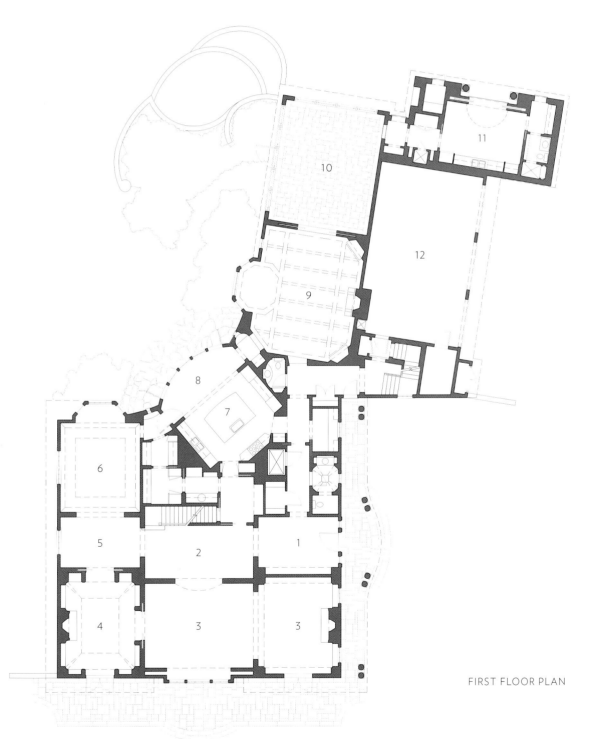

KEY TO FIRST FLOOR
1. ENTRY HALL
2. STAIR HALL
3. LIVING ROOM
4. LIBRARY
5. GALLERY
6. DINING ROOM
7. KITCHEN
8. BREAKFAST ROOM
9. FAMILY ROOM
10. FAMILY PORCH
11. POOL CABANA (BELOW)
12. GARAGE

KEY TO SECOND FLOOR
1. UPPER STAIR HALL
2. MASTER BEDROOM
3. MASTER BATH
4. DRESSING ROOM
5. TV ROOM
6. STUDY
7. BEDROOM

FIRST FLOOR PLAN

0 4 8 16 ft

Left
On the street facade, a broad terrace overlooks the entrance lawn and garden. At night, the double-height bay beneath the gable is a welcoming lantern for visitors.

Left, center and below
A second, broader path, flanked by walled gardens, gently spills from the kitchen's bow window terrace to the pool, a full story below.

Opposite
An axial enfilade extends from the front door to the landscape at the west end of the house. The relatively compressed entrance hall gives way to a cascade of light in the stair hall beyond.

Opposite, below
In contrast to the relatively modest street facade, the east entrance begins to imply a larger house. Above the porch, the master suite's study, TV room and kitchenette overlook the motor court.

Left
The stair hall is bathed in daylight from an elliptical lantern centered above this space. This view, looking back toward the front door and the motor court beyond, suggests a courtyard space that might once have been uncovered.

Opposite
The barrel-vaulted ceiling in the living room provides a parallel double-height space beside the stair hall. An arched opening between the rooms provides borrowed light from the roof-top lantern. The living room is flanked by a wood-paneled library to the west and a lower-ceilinged nook to the east, each with its own fireplace.

Left
This view from the end of the main east/west axis, from the library, shows the dining room, main stair, entrance hall, and front door. For an art-collecting couple, the interior has an appropriate loft-like quality.

Left, below
Our clients' former library was paneled in Australian lace-wood; they wanted to carry that memory into the new house. Our design created opportunities to display both artwork and books. A cross-axial enfilade extends from the library through the main hall to the dining room.

Opposite
The breakfast area off the kitchen has a bow window overlooking the side garden. This room also serves as a "pass-through" between the formal and informal areas, connecting the dining and family rooms.

Opposite

With a nod toward Sir John Soane, the master bedroom is crowned by a handkerchief-vault ceiling. With semi-circular bays on either side of the bed, the room has a purposefully baroque shape, counterbalanced by simple profiles and finishes.

Opposite, below

The TV room, connected to the master study, is detailed in pine with fabric panels and features a tent-like ceiling.

Below

The second-floor bedrooms overlook the pool terrace below as well as the side garden and motor court. Each ceiling is individually shaped, providing rooms that look, feel, and sound different.

Right

The bunk room contains four beds, each with its own light fixture and TV. The snug configuration suggests a Pullman car or ocean liner cabin for a fun kids' journey.

Opposite

The arched window, flanked
by eye-like openings, provides
a engaging backdrop in the
children's playroom.

Opposite, below left

To bring more light into the
pool cabana and introduce a
vertical counterpoint to
an otherwise wide room, we
sculpted a clerestory above
the pocketing doors that open
up to the pool terrace.

Opposite, below right

The kids' back stair connects
their bedroom wing directly with
the playroom, gym and pool
area below.

Below

At the foot of the adults' back
stair, a hall leads to the wine-
tasting room and adjacent wine
cellar. The octagonal space is
paneled in a dark-finished pine.

Left
The beamed ceiling gives the family room a distinct character from other rooms in the house.

Left, below
Wide pocket doors connect the family room to a similarly proportioned porch. In addition to the comfortable, fully furnished sitting area, the family porch can seat forty for an al-fresco summer dinner.

Opposite
The children's playroom, below the family porch and facing the pool, was "discovered" by Douglas Hoerr when he suggested, during construction, that the landscape be "pulled back" to expose the basement and integrate it into the pool terrace and garden. Up above, the main guest bedroom enjoys a Juliet porch, overlooking the pool.

SEASIDE COTTAGE

Founded in the early 1980s, Seaside, Florida, on the Emerald Coast of the Gulf of Mexico, was one of the first communities in the nation to draw on the ideas of New Urbanism to shape its overall design. Modeled on a turn-of-the-twentieth-century beach town, with a traditional town center and abundant community space, Seaside offers a neighborly environment that puts most services within a walkable distance, pursues environmentally responsible construction and land-use policies, and emphasizes regionally appropriate building materials and typologies. Though the residential architectural context remains broadly consistent, with similarly sized lots and building envelopes, visitors find a variety of styles there, many executed by some of America's most talented practitioners.

We were latecomers to the Seaside architectural scene—we created this three-story, 3000-square-foot house a generation after the community began – but the long interval proved beneficial. At its start, Seaside developed slowly, with many of the first

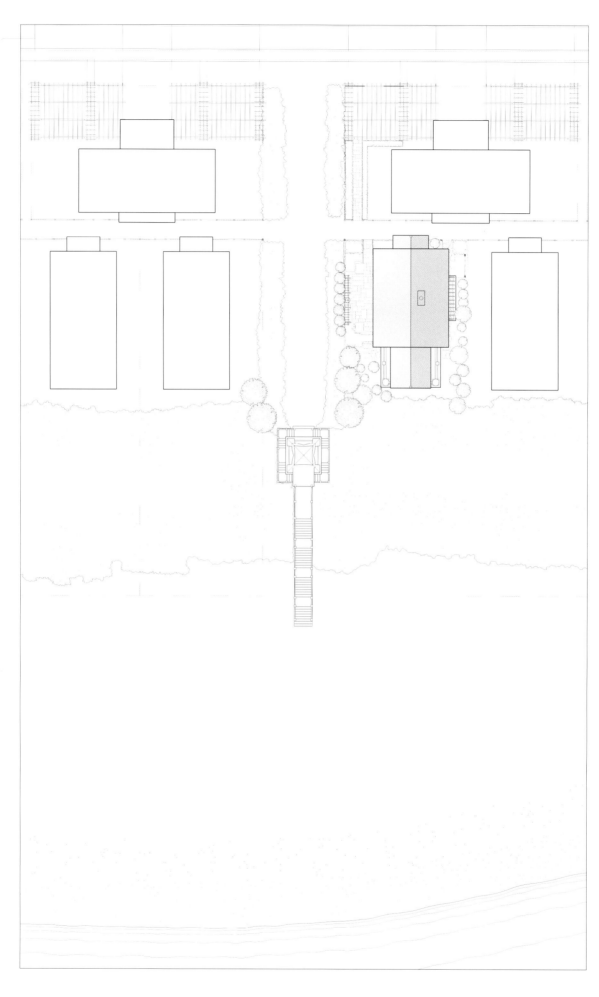

SITE PLAN

0   15   30 ft

residents opting for very modest beach dwellings. With the town's increasing real estate success, the houses became more substantial. The architects and builders, too, grew up with Seaside: the players were able to observe, and learn from, what others were doing, in a design-laboratory environment that educated everyone.

Our clients reflected this model, having owned two previous homes in Seaside, moving ever closer to the water, and ultimately deciding to create a more permanent place on the beach. A well-traveled couple with three children, they were architecturally adventurous, willing to venture outside the regional vernacular styles that had flourished on Seaside's streets. This dovetailed with our interests: arriving at a particular moment in the town's evolution, we hoped to do something that would be recognizably of the place, yet different enough to serve as a model for future local projects.

At the time of this commission, I had recently traveled to Sweden, where I visited Gustavian houses and also buildings revealing the inventive Nordic classicism that flourished in the 1920s. The former, I discovered, were high-style and French-influenced, but stripped down, neutral in color, and of the local vernacular. The Nordic precedents, conversely, were surprisingly playful and innovative in their handling of the classical language. It occurred to me that this might work at the beach—a stylish yet witty classicism that was spare and rendered in simple materials. As it turned out, our clients were aficionados of historic Scandinavian architecture: when I suggested Swedish precedents, they responded with enthusiasm and gave us a largely free hand.

We treated the residence like a townhouse, with rusticated wood at the base and clapboard on the floors above. The pitched roof is covered in pre-patinated copper; custom finials stand poised above paired rafter tails supporting the deep overhanging edges. We incorporated columns into the facades, but they are offset rather than perfectly aligned, and the orders were changed. Greek Tuscan appears on the ground floor, giving way to Doric in the middle and piers on top; on the long entrance facade to the west, a trio of pilasters at the second floor, their capitals carved with a Greek key motif, support a natural pergola. On the narrow north elevation, which faces the town, we set a small pavilion, with roof details echoing those of the main structure and a single Greek Tuscan column, and added a swag detail and a balcony on the facade directly above it.

The south side, with its three stacked porches facing the gulf, is at once the house's most recognizably classical, and strikingly subversive, elevation. The second-floor porch, distinguished by muscular fluted and banded columns, was informed by the work of the highly original nineteenth-century Scottish classical architect Alexander "Greek" Thomson and by Villa Kerylos, an early twentieth-century residence in the Greek style on the Cote d'Azur. The most theatrical gesture is the roof of the third-floor terrace off the master suite, which is undergirded by cedar trusses and held up by a single Ionic column—a classical, Schinkel-influenced composition. We had wanted to create a distinctly iconic moment; this gesture certainly fit the bill, and the clients embraced it immediately.

Above

Inspiration for the composition of the porch off the master suite, with its roof supported by a slender Ionic column came from the spare neoclassicism of Karl Friedrich Schinkel, notably the lone caryatid elegantly supporting the top of a garden pavilion.

The front door is on the west side of the house, at the midpoint of a small courtyard loosely enclosed by native plantings and a pergola; this allowed us to craft a gracious and discreet entry sequence. This side entrance also facilitated a three-bedroom layout as opposed to two: the boy's room, to the left of the entry hall, and a two-bedroom suite for the girls, which opens onto a ground-floor screen porch—complete with custom-designed hanging daybeds—facing the

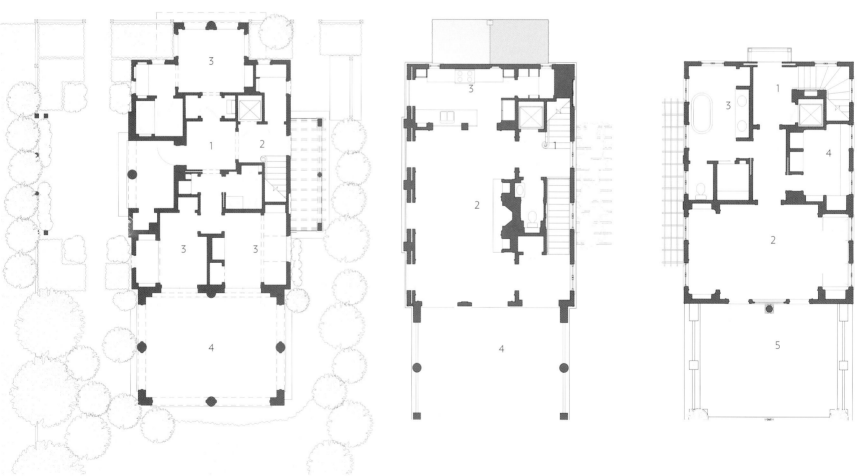

FIRST FLOOR PLAN   SECOND FLOOR PLAN   THIRD FLOOR PLAN

0   5   10 ft

Opposite and right

Despite its proximity to the dunes and the Gulf, the house is close to its neighbors and to the village. Our design, with its enclosed side entrance and substantial water-facing terraces, encourages a sense of privacy and focus on nature.

Overleaf

The grand western elevation, which faces the town, serves as its public space; the north elevation is set on a narrow sand side street and addresses the pedestrian walk. The pavilion, which encloses a child's bedroom, replicates the roof in miniature.

KEY TO FIRST FLOOR
1. ENTRY HALL
2. STAIR
3. BEDROOM
4. SCREENED PORCH

KEY TO SECOND FLOOR
1. STAIR
2. LIVING/DINING ROOM
3. KITCHEN
4. LIVING ROOM PORCH

KEY TO THIRD FLOOR
1. STAIR
2. MASTER BEDROOM
3. MASTER BATH
4. DRESSING ROOM
5. MASTER SUITE PORCH

dunes on the right. A side stair rises to the second-floor living and dining room, with its coffered ceiling and fireplace, an open galley kitchen, and a porch large enough for lounging and al fresco dining, which is accessed via exterior pocket doors. It is a compact plan, but the specificity of detail—the oiled antique pine floors, the custom artwork and hand-carved motif on the mantelpiece—make the room feel grand and gracious despite its small dimensions.

The stair to the third floor arrives at a landing with pocket doors opening onto a Juliet balcony overlooking the town, and a hallway leading to the master suite. The inclusion of a kitchenette, with a bar sink and wine cabinet, allows for entertaining on the suite's private terrace, with its sunset, beach, and water views.

For this small yet highly detailed structure, our master builder likened his task to creating a piece of fine furniture, and his careful approach is reflected in the many elegantly crafted elements that give the residence its special distinction. Whether or not the house influences the next generation of Seaside's residential architecture, it demonstrates that a sense of permanence, the highest level of craft, and a thoughtfully considered reinterpretation of precedents are not incompatible with life at the beach—or expanding the classical canon.

Gary Brewer, Project Partner

Opposite, left
The master bedroom porch, with its single fluted column and covered cedar pergola.

Opposite, right
One of the custom designed and crafted copper roof ornaments.

Below
Details on the east elevation include paired rafter tails and fluted window sills. The ship-lapped boards were influenced by historic houses in Charleston, South Carolina.

Right
The house among its neighbors on Seaside Way—at once fitting in and standing out.

Opposite
The Seaside Way bedroom pavilion features a fluted and banded column with Greek fretwork. The exposed rafter tails and acroteria are carried over from the roof.

Below, left
A custom window grille, set into the rusticated base, is a classical design edged by rosettes.

Below, right
An outdoor beach shower, on the east side of the house, sits beneath a pergola supported by a single column. Our office created the tile design and custom copper lantern.

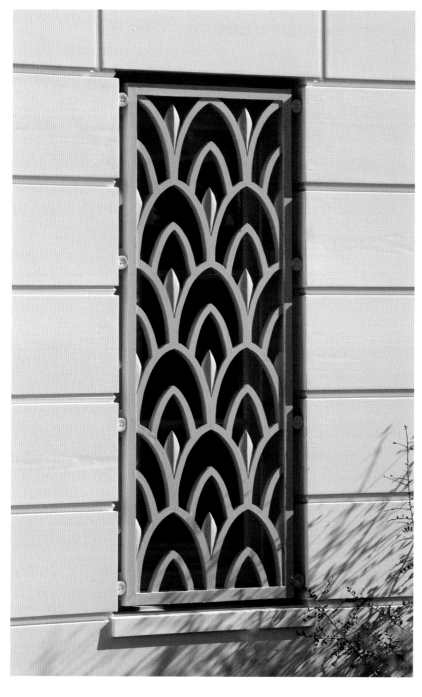

Below
Light from within animates
the exterior architecture
after dark, giving the house
a markedly different, more
theatrical character.

Opposite
The entry incorporates a fluted
Doric column with a banded
base supporting a frieze with
Greek fretwork. The lantern
design references the sea turtles
native to the area.

The living and dining areas are combined in a single, generous space. The central fireplace incorporates built-in cabinets and a new Swedish mural, with panels that conceal a TV; the motif incised above the mural draws on the acroteria on the roof, while the coffered ceiling carries over the beaded board from the walls. Beyond is a "traveling" stair, which rises up from the ground floor through the opening at right and continues upward at left.

Below
Lightly separated from the
open galley-style kitchen by a
pillar with a fluted Greek key
motif, the dining table is set on
axis with the opening to the
stair hall.

Opposite
The acroteria appear again on
the painted wood cabinets in
the kitchen. The pocket doors
open onto a view of the town.

Below
A single Ionic column divides the great picture window, flanked by operable doors in the master bedroom. In a niche opposite the bed is a Swedish-style built-in sofa, flanked by side shelves.

Opposite
The alcove adds a measure of coziness to the sleeping area and, by creating a higher break point for the wall, makes the ceiling feel higher.

Opposite, below left
The custom newel post, crowned by an elegantly turned volute, at the foot of the stair.

Opposite, below right
On the second floor, pocket doors open onto the Juliet balcony overlooking Seaside Way. The hallway connects to the master bedroom.

Left and below
A variant of the exterior rustication enlivens the wall treatment in the entry hall; a crossette at the top of the door casing and a Swedish-style stone floor enrich the architectural character of the small space. Beyond is the snug periwinkle blue pavilion bedroom and its bath.

Opposite
In the master bath, a trayed ceiling elongates the narrow space even as the mirrors above the double vanity, capturing the view, appear to widen it. Swedish detailing appears in the cabinetry; a delicate leaf motif tops the pilasters on the bathtub wall.

Opposite, below left
The pavilion bathroom features a vanity with a fluted detail, set apart from the rest of the space to permit a separation of functions.

Opposite, below right
One of the two girls' bed-rooms, on the opposite end of the ground floor. Both spaces communicate directly with a screened porch that faces the dunes.

Left and below
Both girls' rooms continue the language of boarded walls and ceilings found throughout the house. The television above the built-in chest of drawers is set behind a mirror.

Opposite
In the second girl's room, the bed is set in a Jeffersonian alcove bookended by pilasters; a second trundle bed pulls out from beneath it. The doors to the screened porch incorporate acroteria details.

Overleaf
The ground-floor screened porch, with custom-designed hanging day beds, fluted Doric columns beneath rafter tails, and subtly gradated multi-colored paint scheme, serves as bedroom suite for the girls and opens to the beach dunes.

Opposite

Apart from the drama afforded by a single column on the master suite porch, its central location breaks open the view corridors and encourages diagonal vistas up and down the beach.

Opposite below

The muscular architecture of the living room porch, which easily accommodates dining and sitting areas, includes a beamed ceiling and fluted columns with a Greek key detail. The curtains create a sense of theatre as well as privacy.

Right

Colonette-style pickets flank the single column on the master porch. The volutes on the handrail echo those on the capital above.

ENCINAL BLUFFS FAMILY COMPOUND

The site of this residential compound—a majestic bluff over-looking the Pacific—was both the project's principal attraction and its greatest challenge. The property descends gently to its midpoint, then dramatically falls away nearly ninety feet to the sea. Our clients called for a relaxed home away from home for their extended family, unostentatious and open to the outdoors. While the program suggested a large house, neither the owners nor the topography encouraged us to propose a single massive block. Instead, the temperate climate and the interest we shared with our clients in the vernacular architecture of Mediterranean hill towns led us to break up the program into a village-like com-position of smaller structures. In so doing we created a sunny and sensuous environment evocative of its old-word inspiration, yet very much at home on the California coast.

Those arriving by car enter a narrow drive, reminiscent of an Andalusian village street, and descend to a circular court—an homage to Wallace Neff's Mediterranean Revival architecture—

Opposite
The guest cottage is the most remote outpost of the Mediterranean "hill town" we conceived for this dramatic site. Ocean waves lap the terrace walls at high tide.

wrapped by the compound's largest structure. Informally dubbed the "Cook House," it contains a living room, a dining room, a library, two guest suites, the kitchen, and service facilities. To the east, a broad lawn with a deep loggia along its northern edge plays the part of the village square, an edgeless swimming pool at its center. Across the lawn, a somewhat smaller building (the "Bunk House") accommodates the master suite and the clients' studies. The Bunk House opens onto its own private outdoor rooms: a long terrace overlooking the ocean, an enclosed garden off her bath and dressing room, and a large walled entry court centered on a fountain. A full story up the slope and to the north, a broad set of steps leads down from a gate off the main road to a parterre overflowing with Mediterranean plantings; west and south of this garden are structures for additional guest suites, an exercise room, and a garage.

Interior architectural elements also evoke a Mediterranean vernacular: wood ceilings and plank doors with antique patina, pigmented and waxed plaster walls, and antique stone floors in the entertaining rooms that give way to wide-plank oak floors in the bedrooms and other private spaces. By contrast, galvanized steel casements and French doors update a regional aesthetic and technology originally popular in the 1920s and 1930s, with framing members that are slender enough to allow virtually uninterrupted views, yet strong enough to permit the sash to fold back accordion-style to open the principal rooms to the outdoors.

At a corner of the main lawn, an elevator provides access to a manicured lower terrace with its own horizon-edge pool; steps and pathways continue down to a cottage, built on the footprint of a pre-existing lifeguard's shack, and from there to the beach. In fact, the success of the project hinged in part on the elevator, without which access to the beach would have been difficult. Together with landscape designer Deborah Nevins, we secured permission to excavate for the elevator by producing plans to restore the protected cliffside. The effort was well worth it, as the entire project depended to some extent on the ability to bring people—and food—down to the beach.

As it does so often in the Mediterranean villages that inspired us, water plays an important and recurring role in the story that unfolds as one progresses through each building, and from one part of the compound to the next. Originating in the mountains to the north, an implied natural watercourse seems to flow through the site and resurface periodically in fountains and pools in courtyards, and in basins at doorways as it finds its way to the sea. In addition to sustaining the project's underlying narrative, the various water features cool the air around them on hot days and mask the sounds of the traffic from a nearby highway.

Throughout the compound, we stayed clear of the overly specific expression that characterizes so much of California's contemporary Mediterranean Revival architecture, drawing inspiration instead from a broad range of vernacular Italian, French, and Spanish farmhouses and villages. Volumes and rooflines are simple, unbroken, and additive. The Italian clay tile on the roofs and French stone on the terraces were each reclaimed from a single source, giving the compound a consistency that affirms it is in fact a private house; we were careful not to overplay the village metaphor. Early in construction we visited quarries around the Vaucluse in search of possible stones for the rubble masonry walls and built mockups incorporating these as well as a few domestic stones. In the end a limestone from Texas was a close match in scale, color, and even geology to the creamy samples from the French town of Gordes, and this was used throughout the project.

Above
During construction, a mock-up of a typical building wall included rubble stone from quarries in France and the United States placed side-by-side so we could compare them in the light of the California sun.

Opposite
The narrow drive descending to the Cook House incorporates elements of the vernacular architecture found along streets in European villages such as the Andalusian hamlet at left.

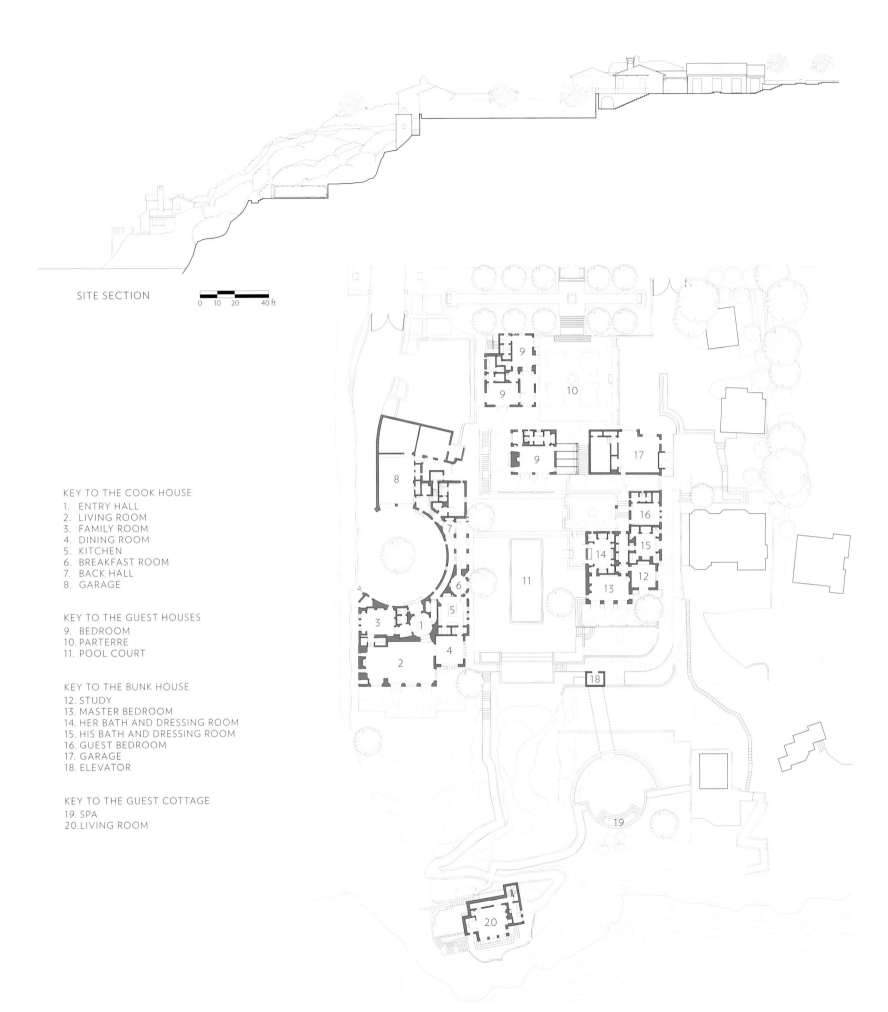

SITE SECTION

KEY TO THE COOK HOUSE
1. ENTRY HALL
2. LIVING ROOM
3. FAMILY ROOM
4. DINING ROOM
5. KITCHEN
6. BREAKFAST ROOM
7. BACK HALL
8. GARAGE

KEY TO THE GUEST HOUSES
9. BEDROOM
10. PARTERRE
11. POOL COURT

KEY TO THE BUNK HOUSE
12. STUDY
13. MASTER BEDROOM
14. HER BATH AND DRESSING ROOM
15. HIS BATH AND DRESSING ROOM
16. GUEST BEDROOM
17. GARAGE
18. ELEVATOR

KEY TO THE GUEST COTTAGE
19. SPA
20. LIVING ROOM

FLOOR PLAN

I cannot overstate the importance of Deborah Nevins to the success of this project. Deborah coordinated the complex grading and drainage and orchestrated the reconstruction of the bluff. She designed and specified the extensive gardens and plantings throughout the compound, and worked with us to detail and execute the sequence of water features. Her understanding of and respect for architecture and its relationship to its surroundings informs her design approach and allows our various buildings to take ownership of the land elegantly and artlessly.

Roger Seifter, Project Partner

Above
The major part of the compound is organized around the pool court. An elevator—or, alternatively, a series of meandering paths—brings people down the bluff to a circular, manicured lawn where they can descend further to the guest cottage and the beach.

Overleaf
From the second-floor terrace, guests at the Cook House can appreciate the full sweep of the motor court as they look out towards the ocean. While the varied roofscape covers a single structure, it suggests a picturesque cluster of separate buildings.

Above and opposite, top
Full-height wooden gates
open the main courtyard
of the Bunk House to the
pool court and to ocean
breezes. A loggia descends
along the opposite side
toward the building entrance.

Opposite, below, left to right
Ironwork details such as this
window grate follow Spanish
colonial traditions as well as
the European vernacular; the
master bedroom terrace
looks across the pool court to
the Cook House; guest rooms
at the upper level open off an
informally planted parterre.

Below, left
On cool nights a fireplace—
and a heated floor—warm
the deep loggia overlooking
the pool court.

Below, right
Toward the east and up a few
steps, the loggia opens to
the common path between the
Bunk House and its garage.

Below

The pool is the center of our "town square." As much an architectural feature as an amenity, it provides a formal order to a picturesque composition by organizing the buildings and spaces around it.

Opposite and below
A monitor in the entry hall of the Cook House brings additional daylight into this mostly interior space. The ceiling establishes a material palette of antique stained wood planks and beams that is used throughout the compound.

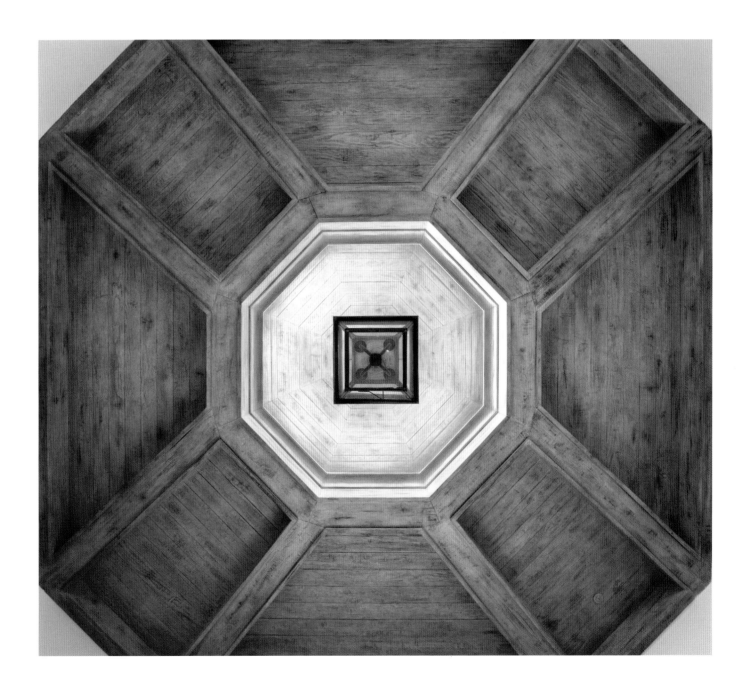

Below
The primary focus of the living room is the ocean view through eleven-foot-high arched doors. So as not to compete, the fireplace is set into a far wall, in its own alcove.

Opposite
The complex geometry of the dining room ceiling draws on traditional Portuguese examples. When the steel-frame doors fold back on themselves, the space transforms into a loggia off the terrace outside.

Opposite
The breakfast room obtains considerable drama from its pitched and paneled ceiling.

Below, right
The kitchen recalls the "fitted" rooms of the 1920s, in which each bank of built-in cabinets is detailed as a separate piece of furniture.

Below
Oak paneling distinguishes the family room from the others and gives it a feeling of warmth appropriate to its use as library and den.

Left
The back hall in the Cook House quite literally follows the curve of the motor court, adding interest and variety to an everyday space and its function.

Below, left
In many instances, the slope of the land is expressed in short runs of shallow steps; arrival at landings is lent significance by windows and other architectural elements.

Below, right
Each of the guest baths has the amenities of a luxury resort along with an architectural twist, such as the curved wall in the Cook House.

Opposite
Simple volumes and plain plaster walls characterize secondary rooms such as the larger bedroom in the Cook House; ceiling detail and strategically positioned doors and windows give these spaces their formal order and repose.

Below, right

In the Bunk House, master bath and dressing are combined in separate facilities for him and her. His space is oak-paneled, with closets on three sides; the vanity mirror pockets into the wall to reveal a window looking onto a bougainvillea-covered trellis, and a corner window in the shower offers a view of the ocean.

Below

This guest room in the Bunk House has direct access to the courtyard.

Left
In her master bath and dressing room the ceiling and walls are paneled in lime-washed oak. Windows and doors around the tub open onto a private walled garden.

Below
The limestone fireplace and trumeau in the master bedroom are set against a short wall to emphasize their presence in the space without compromising the view from the bed. Small windows at each end of the room allow for natural cross-ventilation.

Opposite
His study occupies a prime position off the master bedroom, with ocean views through tall arched doors on two walls. Rising to 13 feet, the pitched ceiling provides considerable architectural impact in a relatively modest space.

Below and opposite
The elevator concealed within
the bluff opens onto a geo-
metrically precise grass terrace
and a direct view of the ocean.
Fragments of antique stone
columns are placed at each end
of the hemicyclical wall that
retains the hillside.

Below
The last leg of the path to the
guest house and the beach
twists down the hillside from
the grass terrace above.

MAISONETTE IN CHICAGO

Having lived for forty years in suburban Illinois, our clients decided to embark on a new life in Chicago, purchasing a duplex in a structure reminiscent of a nineteenth-century Parisian apartment building a block from Lake Michigan. Yet their choice of a maisonette with its own facade and front door several steps up from the sidewalk behind a broad planted bed, suggested that the couple remained attached, and understandably so, to the privacy and independence associated with a freestanding dwelling. Indeed, they appreciated the benefits of a full-service building—and have come to use the back door, accessed from the lobby via a first-floor corridor, more frequently than their street entrance.

The pair specifically requested that we replicate certain aspects of their previous residence, notably a large and much loved pine-paneled library. I characterize the apartment's style as "Franglish," an amalgam of the exterior architecture's beaux-arts aspirations, the couple's Anglo-influenced former residence, and their larger

Opposite
In the entry hall the painted paneling, a generous cove at the ceiling borders, and the patterned floor of Cotswold stone and black granite reflect a mix of French and English influences.

Below
A private entrance, with a garden
buffering it from the sidewalk,
gives the maisonette the quality
of a townhouse.

Opposite
The entrance hall is the core
of the apartment opening
to all first floor rooms and the
elegant stair.

Below, left

In the entry, English antiques, a suite of Japanese prints, and Chinese porcelain from the owners' collections immediately establish a sense of place. The arch above the front door is echoed in the opening to the gallery across the space.

Below, right

The stair rail echoes a design by Sir John Soane. The lamp-filled niches replicate a detail at Claridge's in London.

Opposite

The pine-paneled library recalls a similar space in the couple's previous residence. Radiused corner cabinets make the room feel more discrete and enveloping.

Below
The living room was designed to incorporate a Coromandel screen from our clients' collection.

Right
At the other end of the living room, we extended the radius of the corner bay with the interior architecture. Sculpted plaster mouldings reinforce the room's robust authority.

Opposite
Wall panels in the formal
dining room are finished in an
embroidered silk.

Below
The kitchen incorporates a
small but comfortable breakfast
area and—in a nod to French
influences—a zinc range hood
and island countertop.

Opposite

A delicate latticework cornice in the master bedroom expresses the lighter architectural interpretation on the second floor. French doors connect the space to an adjoining sitting room.

Below

The dressing room features mirrored French doors and a packing table in the center. Crystal drawer pulls add sparkle to the space.

Left
The mosaics on the floor of the master bath were inspired by the remarkable fourth-century examples at Villa Romana della Casale in Sicily.

Opposite
Aquamarine marble pilasters ring the elliptical master bath with its cove-lit ceiling; both the tub and vanity respond to the shape of the room. Backlit panels of milk glass, fitted with polished nickel, frame the mirrors.

Below
Circular in plan, the master
sitting room is a showcase
for a selection of the couple's
Audubon prints.

Below
The narrow master study
features a shallow vaulted ceiling
accented with cove lighting,
which gives the space the flavor
of a gallery.

Left and below
The maisonette includes two
guest rooms with ensuite baths.

Opposite
The second-floor landing, with
its strongly articulated aperture
framing the stairwell, is generously proportioned to enhance
the domestic character of
the apartment.

HOUSE ON HOOK POND

This residence represents a collaboration of sorts between our client and the previous owners, whom he in fact never met—a dialogue across time between sympathetic personalities, with a shared attraction to clarity, authenticity, and a well-articulated sense of place.

The original house, a modest cottage on a two-acre site in East Hampton, was home for sixty-two years to the Norwegian-American painter Claus Hoie and his wife, Helen, a textile artist. Hoie, a watercolorist with a particular attraction to whaling and the shifting perspectives and infinite minutiae of nature, created, across the decades, a singular portrait of the East End, in the years when that part of Long Island was still largely farmland. It was a place where a handful of the postwar era's most important artists could find peace and solitude modestly and inexpensively, and East Hampton, as depicted in Hoie's views of the village, meant a life savored largely for the pleasures of land, sea, and work.

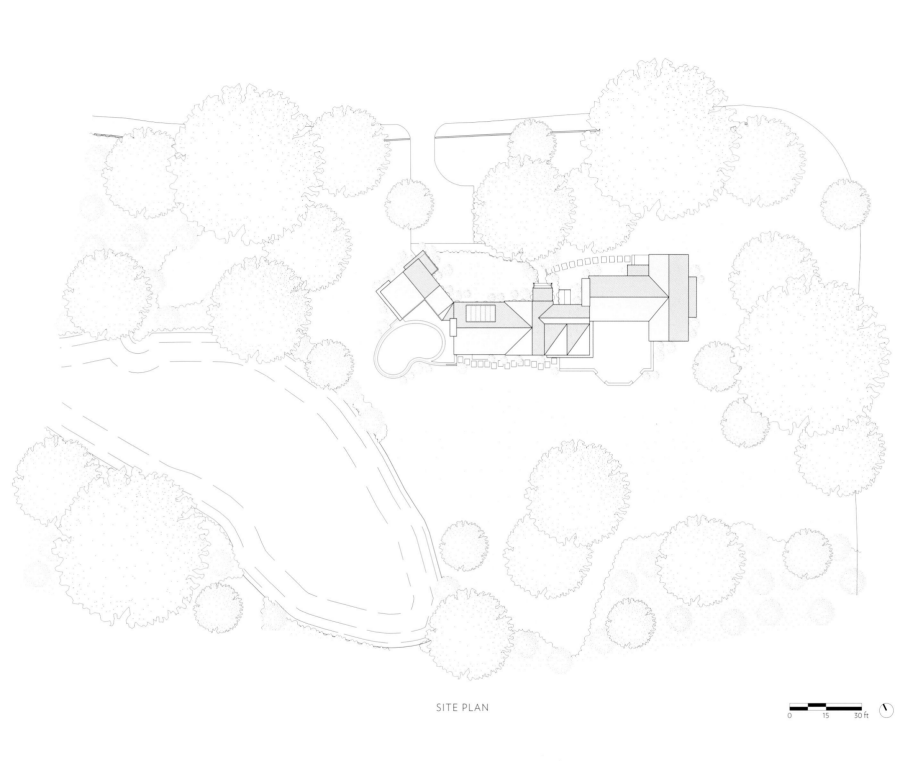

SITE PLAN

0   15   30 ft

Above
The redesigned pond elevation incorporates expansive glazing and, beyond the pool, a new two-story wing. All of the mature trees were retained, and the landscape kept intact.

The Hoies' house, a comfortably utilitarian array of one-story rooms in which the couple lived and worked, reflected this sensibility, as did the property on one of a necklace of ponds connecting to the Atlantic. Though the site, with its sheltering old-growth trees, conveys a sense of seclusion, it is a short bicycle ride to the heart of East Hampton village and, beyond it, the ocean. Following Claus's death in 2006 (Helen predeceased him), the place was sold for a substantial sum, which funded the Helen and Claus Hoie Charitable Foundation, an appropriate conclusion to what, by the early twenty-first century, seemed like a vanished world.

To anyone else, in the overheated real estate market of that time, the house would have qualified as a tear-down. Our client, however, a successful businessman who was also active in the arts as both a maker and a patron, did not need or want a bigger place. Rather, the more he discovered about the Hoies' life and work, the more interested he became in preserving the spirit and character of their home—of blending the particular artistic legacy it represented with a more contemporary aesthetic, one representative of the arts community in his own era.

In this spirit, the structure, which for zoning purposes had to remain within its existing footprint, was not so much reimagined as reprogrammed and enhanced. Claus's studio, a simple board-and-beam shed volume with a peaked ceiling and north-facing atelier-style windows between the rafters, was converted into the living room, with a wall of bookshelves and cabinetry crafted from pine finished to match the existing walls. The flat-roofed dining room remained

in place, though we raised the low ceiling by two feet and added clerestory windows. The adjoining kitchen, which the Hoies had left open to the room, was enclosed and enlarged with space appropriated from closets and a powder room. The original living room became the master bedroom, and its tray ceiling was finished in cedar; adjacent to it, a cluster of small bedrooms served by one small bathroom was transformed into a single open-plan space, half master bath, half dressing area, the two lightly divided by an Asia Pacific-influenced wood screen wall. Throughout, the sash windows on the elevations facing the back yard were replaced, where possible, with broad sliding doors fitted with glass panels, which serve to dematerialize the distinction between house and garden.

Only two substantive changes were executed. Our client requested a pool, which, given the setbacks from the pond, was legally impossible. Robert Stern, however, devised a solution: we removed the last of the Hoies's extensions to the original structure, which held a bedroom, storage area, and extra studio space, and inserted a biomorphic pool into the new—and legitimately buildable—void space. The two-car garage was replaced with a two-story tower, containing a guest bed-and-bath suite below and, on the second floor, a writing studio. In keeping with the residence's history, the tower's geometry is sculptural and abstract, as though conceived by an artist with his own idiosyncratic architectural approach.

An involved client, especially one excited by the prospect of personalizing his home's design, contributes substantively to a project's outcome, and that proved to be very much the case here. Apart from consulting closely with our office throughout design and construction, the owner made his own furniture, fabric, and color selections and engaged the New York artist Jeff Brosk to design a desk and bookshelf for the master suite, the flying saucer-inspired dining table, and several of the residence's doors, all of which add an overlay of custom craft. He also gave his predecessors an unforced yet palpable presence. Works by both Hoies appear throughout the residence; the couple's sofa stands at the foot of a bed, and Claus's painting table, colorfully streaked, remains in the living room, a reminder of the space's original use.

Randy Correll, Project Partner

Opposite

View of the house from the garden prior to renovation. The two-story wing at left, with a painting studio on the ground floor and a bedroom above, was removed to make space for a pool.

Overleaf

Guests are greeted by an entry garden inspired by the owner's visit to Giverny. A new porch shades a former side door, which is now the main entrance. The two-story wing replaced the garage.

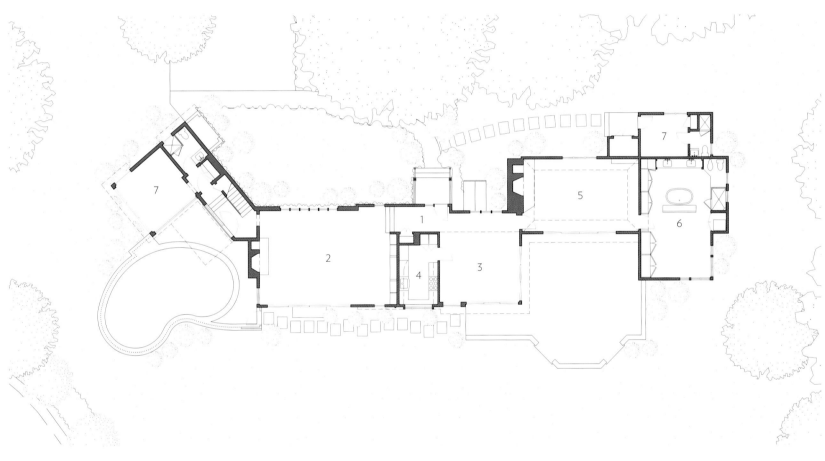

KEY TO FIRST FLOOR
1. ENTRY HALL
2. LIVING ROOM
3. DINING ROOM
4. KITCHEN
5. MASTER BEDROOM
6. MASTER BATH/DRESSING ROOM
7. BEDROOM

FIRST FLOOR PLAN

0   4   8   16 ft

Opposite and below

The asymmetrical roof of the new wing, which encloses a second-floor writing studio and a guest suite on the ground level, suggests the sculptural form of an art studio. To comply with zoning restrictions, the new pool, surrounded by stainless steel pickets, sits within the footprint of what had been part of the house. Raising the pool above grade enabled us to minimize the height of the fence.

The living room was originally the artist's painting studio. To preserve the spirit of creativity, our client filled the room with craft objects, notably woven hanging light fixtures by British designer Russell Pinch and artist Jeff Brosk's coffee table.

Below, left

Our client has collected a number of Claus Hoie's works and keeps the artist's painting table in a corner of the living room.

Below, right

Claus Hoie's watercolor *Skating on Town Pond*, 2003.

Opposite

Although the location of the
dining room remains unchanged,
the ceiling has been raised two
feet. Clerestory windows were
added, as well as sliding-glass
panels on two sides of the room.
Jeff Brosk's "flying saucer" dining
table is surrounded by chairs
that belonged to the Hoies.

Below

The original open kitchen
space was enclosed and fitted
with Pininfarina-designed
cabinetry finished in a peri-
winkle-blue lacquer.

Left
The stair in the new wing features an asymmetrical window that looks out onto the new entry garden. East Hampton lighting designer Marc Figueredo created the chandelier.

Opposite
The second-floor writing studio overlooks the pond and rear landscape. Claus Hoie designed the colorful rug.

RESIDENCE IN NAPA COUNTY

Our clients for this family retreat, set on twenty-four virgin acres along a narrow ridge halfway between Yountville and St. Helena, requested a house planned for easy California living that would evoke time spent with their children in Provence. This seemed entirely appropriate. Napa Valley and the south of France share a common climate—hot dry summer days and cool, even chilly, summer nights—and the rustic gentility of the vineyards and farmhouses scattered over Napa's craggy hillsides likewise recalls the landscapes of Provence.

We carved a winding drive into the steep slope with sweeping views of the valley; the house and its outbuildings are concealed until a final bend reveals a terraced landscape near the top of the ridge. The pool house, in the foreground, is nestled into the hillside, while the main house and garage, above it, frame two sides of an implied courtyard beyond. As the land rises steeply from the pool to the front door of the house, we tempered the climb with landscape elements that subtly tie the buildings together.

COMPOUND PLAN

0   75   150 ft

Above
We were inspired by the vernacular Provencal farmhouses that had charmed our clients as well as California's Mission and Rancho Revival architecture. A specific precedent is the Meyer Ranch in Santa Barbara by Gordon B. Kaufmann to which our house relates in form and materials.

The main house, connected to the garage by a high garden wall, is set on a podium of broad grass steps that descend gently to the motor court to the north and to the vineyard above the pool house to the east. Stone walls and stairs lead from the house to the pool. Terraced rows of olive trees between the pool and the drive complete the ensemble and imbue it with a serene sense of place.

As the valley vista to the northeast was relatively undifferentiated and noisy, we set the main body of the house near the site's southwest edge and oriented the major rooms, bathed in warm afternoon light, toward the more dramatic views in that direction. The picturesque massing was inspired by the vernacular villages and farm groupings dear to our clients: simple gabled roofs abut one another with seeming randomness, their peaks sometimes aligned and sometimes at right angles. We reinforced the romantic character by varying the sizes of the volumes and staggering eaves and roof ridges to express the hierarchy of the rooms within; chimneys punctuate the composition in the manner of Mediterranean and Spanish Colonial campaniles.

The programmatic heart of the house, and the center of family activity, is a combined family room and kitchen, which we located in the largest and tallest volume, with two children's bedrooms above. The balance of the house extends on one level from either end of this mass, with each of the principal rooms under its own gable. The master bedroom overlooks the pool to the southeast and the ridge to the west; at the opposite end of the house, the nearly freestanding living room opens on two sides to the views and on the third side to a walled garden. Linking these volumes is a gallery, held tight along one edge of the house as a buffer against the valley and fully open to the family room. A series of French doors leading from the gallery to a broad terrace to the east brings ample morning light into the west-facing public rooms.

The materials and colors of the house evoke the spirit of Provence, in some cases quite literally. Our clients found the ochre pigment that impregnates the stucco walls in the Luberon; mixed in with the Portland finish coat, it gives the house a saturated but authentically uneven effect. The roof tiles, reclaimed from France and Italy and installed unrestored, give the house an aged texture. Other materials are decidedly local and reinforce the house's relation to its site and California's own architectural traditions. The interiors overlay their French farmhouse inspiration with influences from vernacular adobe construction and its distillation through the Mission Revival.

Details are drawn with geometric simplicity and consistency. Strong walnut lintels at thick door and window surrounds obviate the need for moldings and help create an impression of masonry walls in spite of their actual frame construction. Ceilings (when not plaster) and beams are built

from stained fir, extending up into the pitch of the roofs. Steel doors and windows are rooted in the industrial sash characteristic of California's modernist and traditional architecture of the 1920s and 1930s. Together with screened panels that pocket fully into the walls, the thin frames of these units, which fold flat against the house when opened, promote an effortless flow between inside and out.

The pool house perhaps best embodies the modest attitude of this project towards its site. Comprised of two guest rooms connected by a trellised outdoor living room, the pool house is sunk into the hillside and invisible from the main house. Faced in local rubble stone, it is treated as a retaining wall rather than as a stand-alone four-sided structure. We intended the main house to be similarly unobtrusive: massed to reduce its overall scale, its low silhouette follows the curves of the land. The terraces surrounding the house transition easily to the manicured grounds that, in turn, blend into the untouched landscape beyond, blurring the distinction between the man-made and the natural.

Roger Seifter, Project Partner

Opposite

The first view of the house
and outbuildings as the drive
rounds its final bend: the
poolhouse is in the foreground
with the main house and
garage beyond.

Overleaf

A small vineyard buffers the
main house from the gravel
motor court and garage. The
composition of adjacent
gabled volumes of varying
heights and alignments,
punctuated here and there by
campanile-like chimneys, is
intentionally picturesque yet
respects the hierarchy of the
spaces within.

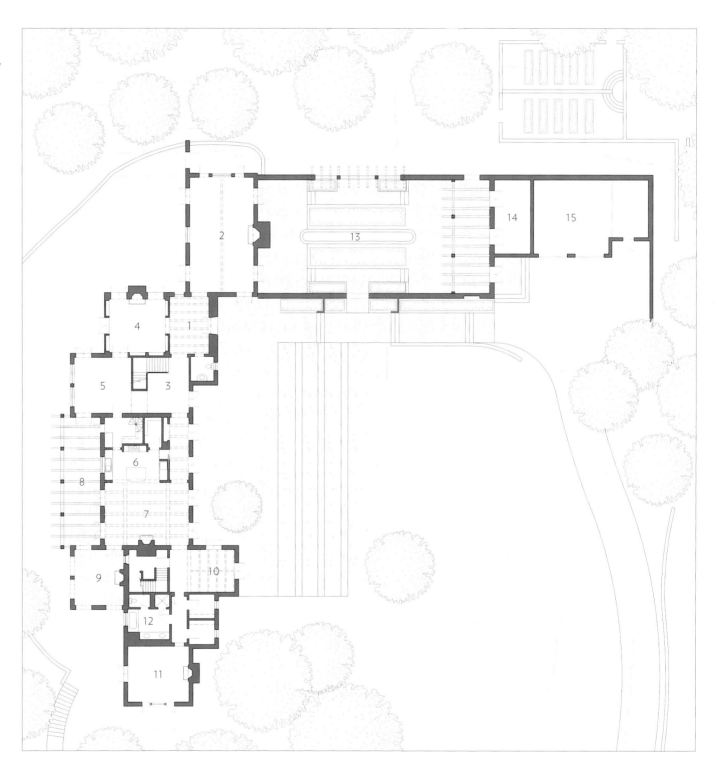

KEY TO FIRST FLOOR
1. ENTRY HALL
2. LIVING ROOM
3. MAIN STAIR
4. LIBRARY
5. DINING ROOM
6. KITCHEN
7. FAMILY ROOM
8. PERGOLA
9. PORCH
10. BREAKFAST ROOM
11. MASTER BEDROOM
12. MASTER BATH
13. WALLED GARDEN
14. GYM
15. GARAGE

FIRST FLOOR PLAN

0 5 10   20 ft

Below
The stepped stone path along-
side the living room garden
wall, leading to the front door.

Right

In its own gabled pavilion set perpendicular to the main body of the house, the breakfast room opens east and south onto a gravel terrace at the head of a series of broad grass steps.

Right, center and below

A terraced garden, set apart from the entry side of the house by a high wall, extends east from the living room. Stepped pathways and a cascading center rill descend towards a pergola and exercise room adjoining the garage at the far end.

Overleaf

Organized around a limestone fireplace, the porch on the west side of the house opens off the family room. Beyond is a dining terrace paved in the same Santa Barbara sandstone.

Below

The refectory-like living room is suffused with daylight on three sides through arched doors and windows; the fir-paneled ceiling and spare plaster walls enhance its monastic character. The steel-frame doors and windows used throughout the house provide maximum sightlines and a note of modernity.

Opposite
Consistent with the house's anecdotal character, the end of the living room looks out on the view through the "ruin" of a masonry arch that suggests a grander structure that might once have been.

Right
In the family room, a lower, beamed ceiling and cabinetwork grouped around a battered rubble stone fireplace recall the Mission Revival as well as Arts and Crafts styles.

Below
The breakfast room is in fact a large alcove off the gallery, distinguished by its gabled ceiling and arched door overlooking the Napa Valley.

Below
The core of the main floor is
a series of spaces that flow
easily from one to the other
with few walls intervening;
the rhythm of ceiling beams
defines specific areas and
paths of circulation. Openings,
such as this oval window, extend interior sight lines toward
the view.

Opposite and below

Set apart from the core of the house as more discrete spaces, the dining room and library break with the prevailing architecture of the interior, but in different ways. The gently arched dining room ceiling sets a quiet and serene stage for the expansive view through its wall of fixed tall windows. The library is focused inward, on its fireplace and books. With walls and ceiling fully paneled in cherry, it is the most formally detailed room in the house.

Left
The master bedroom, at the far
end of the main level, enjoys
unique and private views to the
west and south.

Left and opposite
The pool house is partially buried into its hillside in order to minimize its intrusion on southerly views from the main house beyond. Essentially a retaining wall whose local rubble stone cladding is a visual counterpoint to the ochre stucco of the house, this "non-building" blends naturally and seamlessly with the surrounding landscape.

HOUSE AT BLUE WATER HILL

This shingle style house occupies a privileged spot atop Blue Water Hill. Once the location of a grand estate, the area was subdivided in the 1960s and small ranch-style houses were built in the ensuing decades, most of which were subsequently demolished as Westport's real estate values escalated. Thanks to its panoramic views of Long Island Sound, our clients, a couple with two children, owned the best lot, but the existing house, at 1,700 square feet, was too small from the day the family moved in. They came to us requesting a shingle residence—one that, despite a considerable increase in size, would express a contrasting discretion.

We began by reversing the most common expectation of a shingle style house—that it have brown shingles. Evoking the name of the area, we specified shingles hand-dipped in blue stain, set off by white shutters and a gray roof. We also decided that the house should suggest the simplicity of the nineteenth-century beach cottages on Nantucket or Mackinac Island rather than

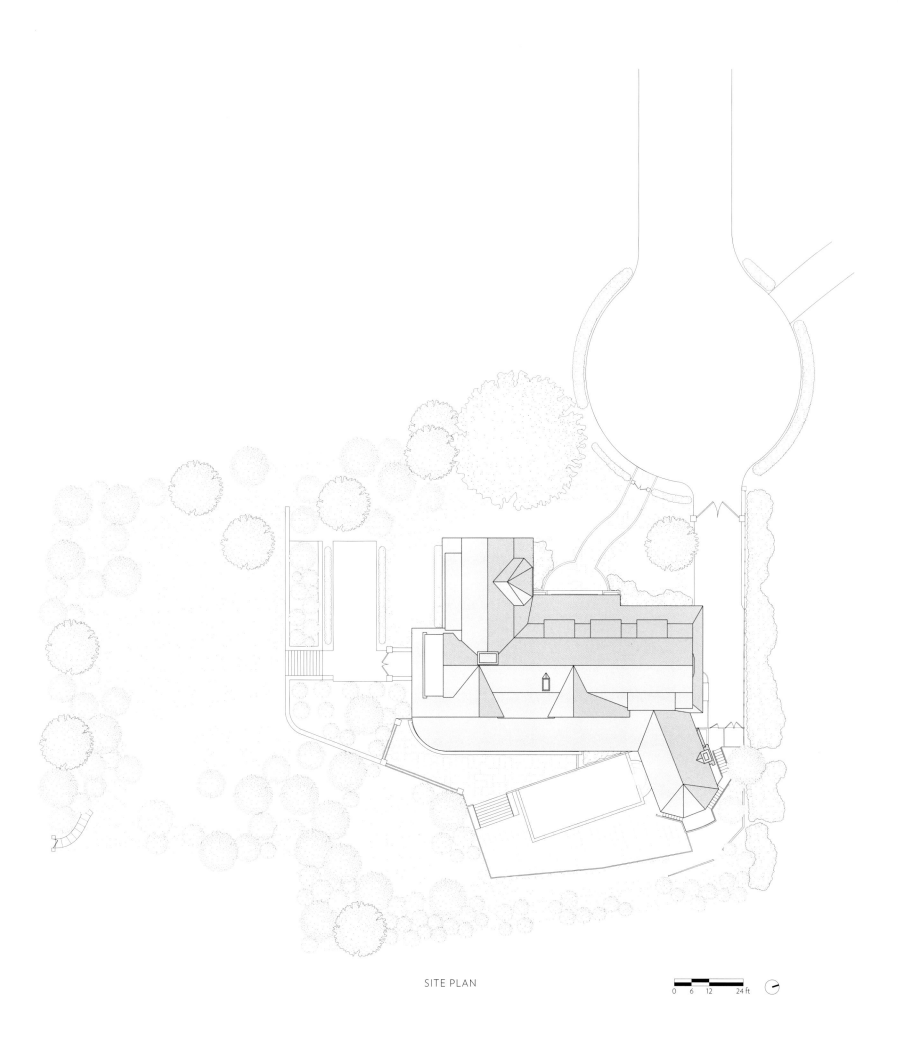

SITE PLAN

0   6   12   24 ft

Above
The house is nestled comfortably within a series of generously scaled green spaces. The siting, plan and envelope were all influenced by local zoning considerations, height limitations, and setback regulations.

making a big statement. Marking the entrance are a white picket fence, three discreetly scaled shed dormers above trelliswork trained up with roses, and a cheerful painted porch.

While the front facade features small double-hung windows and shutters appropriate to the style, we exchanged those on the water side of the house for nearly full-height glazing to capture the magnificent views. Within, we explored our interest in period detail to craft animated surfaces that infuse even the "serious" rooms with exuberance and delight. The entry and stair hall set the tone, with ceiling beams crossing v-joint boards, high wainscoting and robust casings, and classical elements deployed in a freeform manner characteristic of the historic shingle style.

The plan developed primarily in response to the waterside location, and the requirements of a young family. We oriented the major rooms toward the water—the living room with its projecting cylindrical bay, dining room, kitchen, breakfast room (which share a wraparound

porch), and family room are all lined up along the L-shaped perimeter. On the second floor, the master suite and two children's rooms are on the water-facing side of a single loaded corridor arrangement. A fourth bedroom for guests, like the library directly below it, overlooks the side yard.

The main level is divided into two zones: there are the more formal rooms—the entry/stair hall, living and dining rooms, and the library, which are often used for entertaining—and the more casual suite of spaces in which parents and children typically spend most of their time, i.e., the kitchen, and breakfast and family rooms. The master suite is set above the public areas because they are quieter, and is accessed via the main stair; the kids' rooms are over the informal zone, and a secondary 'back' stair links them to it. The American preference for open-plan living saves the two halves from Balkanization: a strong visual connection dissolves the divide, as does the shared view.

Ordinarily, when architects discuss contextualism, the conversation focuses on design—that is, how a new building will relate, aesthetically, to its surroundings. Here we concerned ourselves with contextualism of a different sort. As is often the case in highly desirable communities with much sought-after building sites, the project came with challenges – planning and zoning conditions, height limitations and setbacks—that, taken together, had a significant impact upon our design. Yet with thoughtful planning and imagination, we were able to answer all of Westport's contemporary requirements while still producing a modern family house that would have been entirely at home in an earlier century.

Gary Brewer, Project Partner

SECOND FLOOR PLAN

0 5 10 20 ft

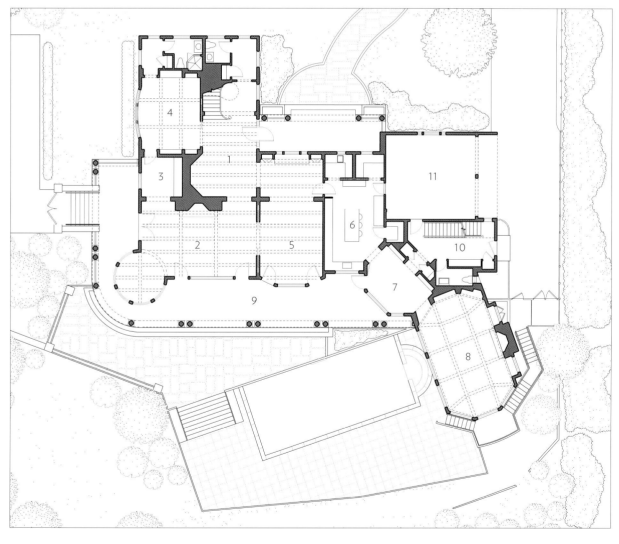

KEY TO FIRST FLOOR
1. ENTRY HALL
2. LIVING ROOM
3. BAR
4. LIBRARY
5. DINING ROOM
6. KITCHEN
7. BREAKFAST ROOM
8. FAMILY ROOM
9. PORCH
10. FAMILY STAIR
11. GARAGE

KEY TO SECOND FLOOR
1. LANDING
2. MASTER SITTING ROOM
3. MASTER BEDROOM
4. MASTER BATH
5. DRESSING ROOM
6. BEDROOM
7. TERRACE

FIRST FLOOR PLAN

0 5 10 20 ft

Opposite and below

With its cheerful white picket
fence enclosing a garden, trio
of shed dormers, trelliswork,
and simple painted porch, the
entry facade evokes the welcoming qualities of a nineteenth-
century waterside cottage.
Indeed, the grandest element
on view is the weeping beech
that is the property's prize.

Opposite

The front door is framed by
custom leaded side lights
and a transom, which create
a welcoming entry. A large
elliptical casing and bold
pilaster frame the stair.

Below

The entry hall, with its beamed
ceiling, high wainscot and strongly
cased openings, connects
the library and living and dining
rooms, and, with its piano,
is itself used for entertaining.

Left and below
Directly opposite the front door, the library also serves as a billiards room. A faux bookshelf door decorated with the spines of imaginary volumes opens onto the bar.

Below, left
The bar, which opens to both the library and living room, is also an entertaining space and game room.

Opposite
The dining room, which incorporates a cork-finished ceiling with a herringbone pattern, can be closed off from the living room with pocketing oak doors.

Left
The breakfast room, between
the family room and the
kitchen, overlooks the porch
and Long Island Sound.

Below
In the kitchen, white tile, marble
countertops, and glass-fronted
cabinets all evoke an earlier era.

Below
In the family room, the tall octagonal trayed ceiling captures the space beneath the roof.

Below
The living room continues the
motif of ceiling beams crossing
V-joint boards. The custom
mantelpiece draws the attention
inward; fully glazed walls open
to the expansive views.

Opposite
A curved corner alcove makes
the living room a space that
can host both larger gatherings
and intimate conversations.

Opposite
In the hallway of the children's suite, custom-designed work areas are set in the dormers overlooking the entry garden.

Below, left
French doors connect the master bedroom to an ensuite sitting room with a wood-burning fireplace.

Below, right
The trayed ceiling in the master bathroom received a glazed finish reminiscent of the inside of a conch shell. A modest claw-foot tub and painted wood cabinetry balance the ceiling's glamour.

Below

The corner guest room draws
on the roof form to give it
architectural interest. Opposite
the bed is a built-in chest of
drawers beneath a mirror.

Left
The curved bay off the living room enables the porch to turn the corner gracefully, while the roof's exposed beams and rafter tails sustain a lively cadence.

Below
A hydrangea-lined path extends from the beach to the west side of the house and the great weeping beech beyond.

Opposite
The long painted porch, with exposed rafters and custom light fixtures, spans the living and dining rooms and looks across the pool to the sound. The family room, at the end of the pool, is its own pavilion and connects to the main block of the house through the breakfast room and kitchen.

WEST VILLAGE TOWNHOUSE

It is unusual to be able to say that you've known a client since he was twelve years old, but that is in fact the case with Robert Stern's son, Nick. Our friendship dates from the 1980s, when I worked with Stern *père* on his own East Hampton country home, and Nick was often in residence. Twenty five years later, when Nick and his wife, Courtney, an interior designer, found a Greek Revival townhouse in Manhattan's West Village for their growing family (which now includes three children), I was asked to continue my collaboration with the Sterns and help the couple give new life to their historic residence.

The townhouse, which dated from the mid-nineteenth century, had much to recommend it, notably its scale. New York townhouses are typically quite narrow, but this one is twenty-five feet wide, which meant that its three-story side stair didn't impinge on the graciously proportioned living spaces. The challenge lay in the fact that the house had been divided into apartments and, after decades of neglect, little of the original could be salvaged.

Opposite

The master suite vestibule, which connects the bedroom to the private deck overlooking the garden, measures only five by six feet. But by adding a robust chest with family photographs, a big chandelier, and a bright color, Courtney Stern, who oversaw the interior design, transformed a pass-through space into something singular.

With a relatively clean slate, we all wrestled with finding an appropriate aesthetic language for the renovation. The house had been altered over time, most significantly in the twin living rooms on the parlor floor, which had been refitted with ornate Victorian mouldings after the Civil War. Bob Stern, a historian generally in favor of preserving a structure's architectural layers, felt the changes should largely remain. Yet the pure Greek Revival style has a boldness to its proportions and a classical simplicity that is highly compatible with contemporary art, architecture, and furniture – it lets you have your classicism and eat it too, so to speak. While we all liked the idea of a layered experience, the Victorianism didn't appeal to any of our sensibilities. Instead, we drew on Greek Revival precedents for the essential architecture and then tapped its affinity with twentieth-century design movements to go in different directions—in effect we created our own historical layers. This enabled the Sterns and me to find our way as we went in response to different programmatic and aesthetic considerations.

"Finding our way" produced one of the house's most purely delightful elements, which grew out of the reconfiguration of the basement level to include a bedroom/bathroom suite, new kitchen, and a dining room communicating directly with the rear garden. As it happened, the house had a "tea porch," a two-story pavilion appended to the rear facade, which served as a garden room where the original residents could take afternoon tea. The existing porch contained two rooms, one in the basement, the other at the parlor level, and we decided to reconstruct it as an expansively glazed double-height atrium, with the garden-level dining room accessed from above by a sweeping grand stair—a massive injection of sunlight and glamour. As it represented an opportunity for Bob to research and reinterpret the tea porch typology, this part of the house received intensive study: multiple iterations, featuring different solid-to-glass ratios, were drawn, and the office constructed a large model of the final design. The outcome, supported by the stair's decorative ironwork and Courtney's selection of sconces, offers the Continental flair of a prewar French interior within the larger American context—an environment so inviting that additional furniture was added, as the family now spends much of its time there.

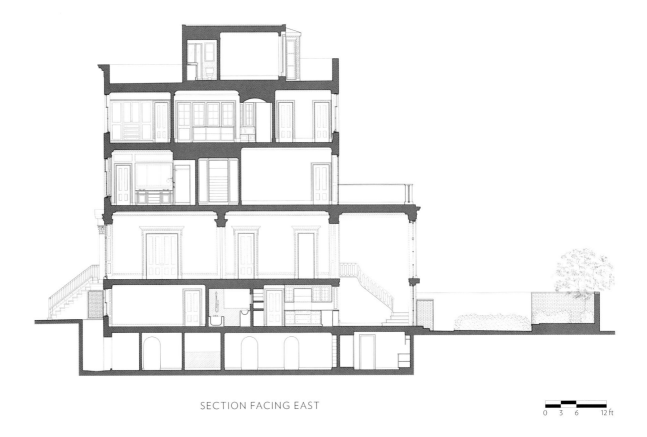

SECTION FACING EAST

0   3   6   12 ft

The parlor floor, with its communicating twin living rooms, retained its original plan, though we replaced the crown mouldings, door casings, and mantelpieces with elements approximating what existed originally. But the floor above—the master suite and Courtney's office—is very different. The bedroom, which opens onto a south-facing terrace atop the tea porch, is entered via a vestibule at the top of the stairs, and connects to an en suite dressing room and, beyond it, the bath. The office can be accessed from either the stair hall or the bath, enabling the couple to move exclusively within their private quarters and avoid the house's public zone. The quiet limestone mantel we designed for the bedroom is a response to the tree-patterned wallpaper, a reproduction of an antique Chinese design, which Courtney selected to draw the garden's serenity into the space. Its presence shifted all of the suite's architecture to a supporting role.

The house's width proved especially beneficial on the children's floor, one flight above their parents. We were able to comfortably fit bedrooms with adjoining baths in both the front and the rear so there was room in the center of the plan for a large shared playroom. The need to bring natural light into this architecturally landlocked space, which necessitated the insertion of windows overlooking the stair hall, directly beneath a skylight, also encouraged us to have fun with the seven-foot-wide, three-story vertical transportation zone. Having been a frequent visitor to the Cleveland Arcade as a child, I have an appreciation of elegant interior public spaces, with tiers of shops and walkways overlooking a central court, and natural illumination

Above, left
The landmarked Greek Revival street facade, which dates from the 1840s, was restored to its original appearance.

Above, right,
Nick and Courtney Stern— joined by Nick's father, Bob— stand in one of the soaring cased openings in the library, which overlooks the double-height atrium on the garden side of the house.

KEY TO GARDEN FLOOR
1. MUDROOM
2. BEDROOM
3. KITCHEN
4. FAMILY ROOM
5. GARDEN

KEY TO PARLOR FLOOR
1. ENTRY HALL
2. STAIR HALL
3. LIVING ROOM
4. LIBRARY

KEY TO SECOND FLOOR
1. STAIR HALL
2. VESTIBULE
3. MASTER BEDROOM
4. DRESSING ROOM
5. MASTER BATH
6. STUDY
7. TERRACE

Opposite

Bob Stern's reinterpretation of the historic "tea porch" typology transformed what was traditionally an unenclosed two-story structure into a semi-glazed double-height space, but retained the bi-level structural template of the original.

Overleaf

The family room opens onto the south-facing garden. A change in level separates the seating and dining areas. Cairo, the family dog, was the only one not to voice an opinion on the design.

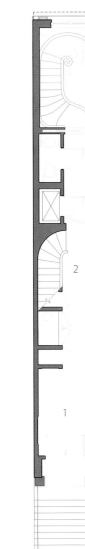

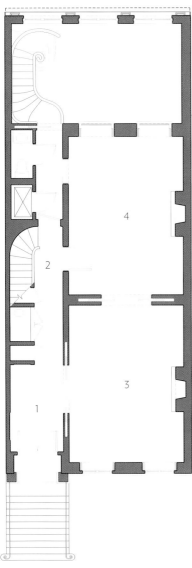

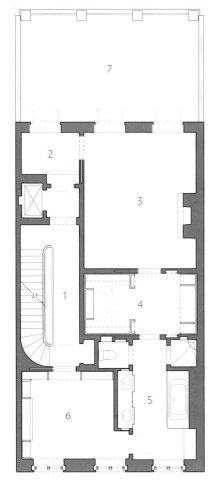

GARDEN FLOOR PLAN

PARLOR FLOOR PLAN

SECOND FLOOR PLAN

0   5   10 ft

filtering down from a skylight. As the stairwell offered a domestic-scale version of this condition, we were inspired to add a windowed turret at the junction of the playroom and the back bedroom that gives a quirky visual flourish when you look up from below and creates a whimsical domed seating area for the kids to enjoy.

With a cellar-level family room and a penthouse guest suite, the house now has six habitable floors, a spatial palette suited to a variety of experiences. No less rich was the interplay between the Sterns and me as we worked our way through the design. A builder by profession, Nick dug into the myriad visual and mechanical details, while Courtney remained more absorbed in the larger narrative; all of us maintained an ongoing dialogue, and Bob consulted on, and contributed to, every phase. And following our noses produced an unexpected outcome: a satisfying architectural unity that remains flexible enough to accommodate changes in the lives of a young and still evolving family.

Randy Correll, Project Partner

Opposite

The front parlor features Greek Revival details that pair sympathetically with modern art and furniture. The colorful and eclectic interior design scheme is reminiscent of a prewar Parisian salon but rendered in a contemporary idiom.

Below

The rear parlor serves as the library. The room sits at the center of the plan but draws abundant light from the double-height family room beyond.

Opposite

The new stair, based on a 1930s French design, cascades with theatrical glamour down from the rear of the parlor floor to the family room. Jean Royere-inspired sconces reinforce the continental atmosphere.

Right

A diptych by Vik Muniz straddles the upper and lower precincts of the atrium. The inner and outer openings, mirroring one another, recall the form of what was once divided into upper and lower floors.

Below
The wallpaper in the master
bedroom, a reproduction
of an antique Chinese paper,
is a fanciful extension of the
garden beyond.

Below
The master dressing room
connects the bedroom to
the bath, which looks onto
the street.

Right
Courtney's comfortable,
well-equipped study can be
accessed from both the
master bath, which it adjoins,
or the stair hall.

Right, below
Mirrored panels visually expand
the master bath.

The Sterns' son enjoys his own room, with a view of the garden; their daughters share a prettily papered space facing the street.

Right
Between the two children's rooms is a spacious playroom, with windows that draw in natural light from the skylight at the top of the stairwell.

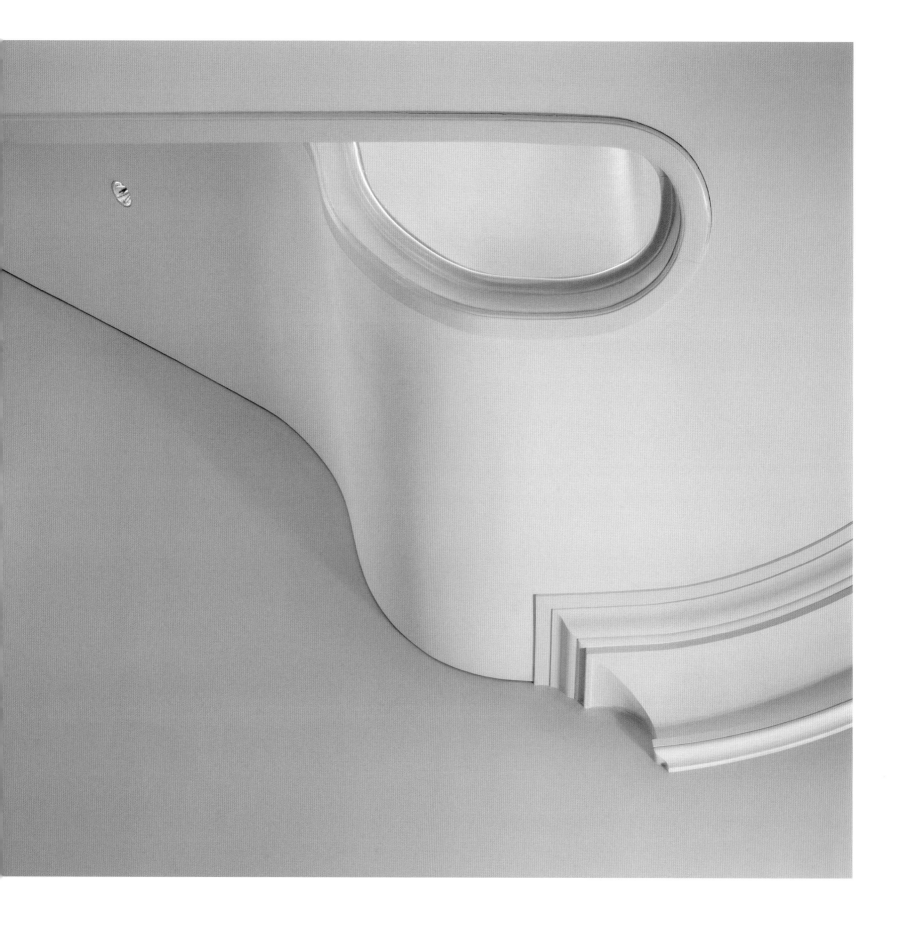

Opposite, below, and right
Because the townhouse was unusually wide, the stairwell is a graciously proportioned space. The "turret" contains a playroom sitting area.

HOUSE ON GEORGICA COVE

If architecture has much to do with responding to existing conditions through the lens of a client's program, this is certainly the case when the project is a renovation, in which the "conditions" are those established by a preexisting house. This project involved expanding a shingle style residence that the owners had built twenty years earlier on a three-acre waterside site with views toward Georgica Pond in East Hampton. The couple wanted to create enough bedroom space to accommodate their two married children and five grandchildren; to enlarge the entertaining spaces and reorganize those reserved for the family; and to make the entire experience, as they put it, more luxe. The ways in which the structure could and could not expand were, to our eyes, fairly apparent. More ephemeral was the task of preserving the character of the house: it was embedded with family memories, and our clients did not want to lose that intimate history.

The building featured an L-shaped plan, with a primary wing, oriented toward the water, containing the main rooms and a

Opposite
In renovating this house, we filled in the area between two gambrels, creating a pedimented entry porch that clearly marks the front door as well as new space on the second floor.

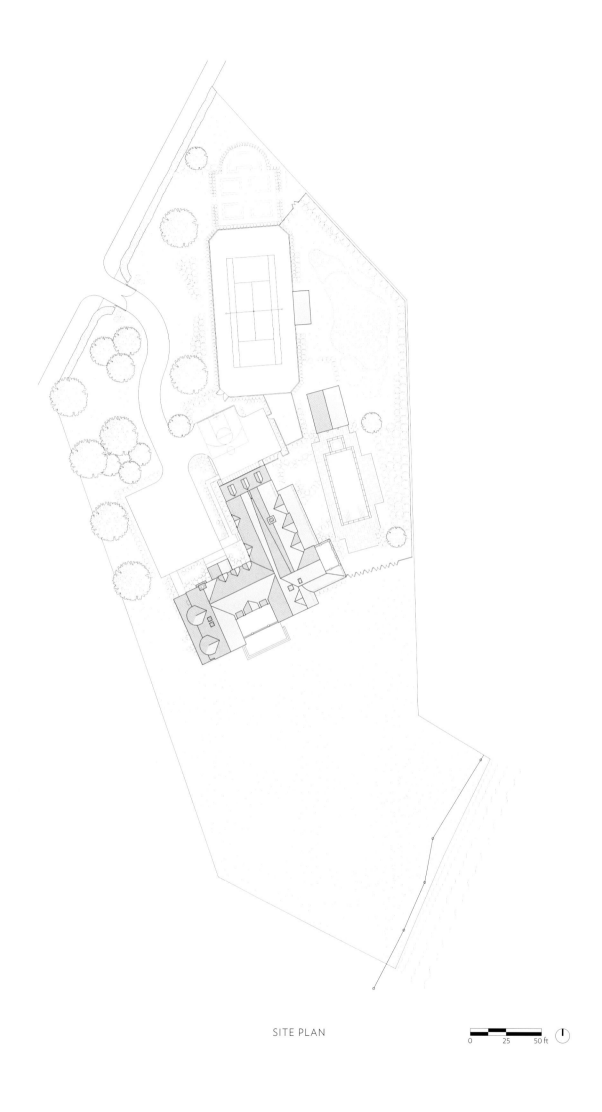

SITE PLAN

0   25   50 ft

service wing between the motor court and the pool. In the former, we enclosed and built over what had been a recessed front porch, making the entry hall deeper and more welcoming, and creating room for the couple's two offices in the new space directly above it. These changes also enabled us to raise the roof at its center, a compositional improvement that filled in an awkward void between two disconnected gambrel shapes, and to move the back door—which had previously been less than twenty feet from the main entrance under the same recessed porch—to the service wing. A pedimented volume became the new front porch.

The library, to the right just past the entrance, was octagonal and thus challenging to furnish. In addition to restyling its interior architecture, we squared off the space, which increased its utility. The living room, beyond the library, remained unchanged. We enlarged the dining room, which like the library lost its chamfered corners, stealing square footage from the adjoining family room to do so. Losing space as well to the adjacent kitchen, the family room became a fully glazed breakfast area. A two-story windowed wall to the left of the hall was reglazed to amplify the light and views. Outside we also connected a series of covered porches along the water-facing side, enlarged the previously unusable screened porch to accommodate a dining table and seating area, and deepened the porch outside the entry hall to make it more comfortable.

When we first saw it, the service wing was a slender amalgam of disparate elements—a small kitchen and breakfast nook, laundry, and storage space—with a garage dangling from a breezeway at the end. Since the east facade, facing the pool, was within setback restrictions, we were able to deepen the entire volume on that side, making space for an enlarged kitchen and communicating family room as well as a children's playroom. We incorporated the garage into the overall design and created a unified, well-composed pool elevation.

On the second floor, the master suite was reorganized to provide a more generous entry and dressing rooms, and the bedroom fenestration was altered to better capture the panoramic view over the water. Two bed-and-bath suites for the couple's grown children were largely unchanged, but the expansion of the service wing allowed a major transformation of the upper floor. This volume became a five-bedroom, four-bath grandchildren's duchy, in which each child has the kind of space, considered architecture, and dedicated closet and bath areas that make family visits a pleasure.

Above

In its original incarnation, the house was more an assemblage of disparate volumes than a unified composition, with the garage loosely appended to the service wing and an awkward void between two disconnected gambrels in the main block. The renovation resolves those issues by raising the roof between the gambrels and integrating the service wing and garage into the building.

Inevitably, given the circumstances, our clients were reluctant to part with certain elements, notably the fireplace and large decorative chimney that obscured the water view in the original family room. We wanted to replace it with French doors, and after much back and forth the couple finally agreed. I urged the builder to remove the object immediately, before they changed their minds, but because the fireplace had to be taken down one brick at a time, the process took months—and the issue of the chimney was revisited week after week.

Yet, ultimately, the additions and subtractions were in sympathy with the original, and most guests familiar with its first incarnation remark that the house seems improved, but can't quite articulate what the difference might be. Happily, the owners feel the same way. "When we look at the old pictures, even though the place is very different now, it still has the old qualities, we don't feel like we've moved into a new home," our client has observed. "It was a nice little place, quaint and quirky. Now it's a real, adult family home—the house grew up."

Randy Correll, Project Partner

Opposite

On the water-facing elevation, we united the two gambreled roofs by filling the space between them and added a gabled dormer to mark the center. The first-floor porches are now continuous, and the expansive picture windows are flanked by French doors or double-hung windows with panes—a modern approach to the shingle style.

Overleaf

Seen from across the cove the house has the relaxed, rambling quality of the shingle style. The reconfigured east wing overlooks the pool and gardens.

SECOND FLOOR PLAN

0 5 10   20 ft

KEY TO FIRST FLOOR
1. ENTRY HALL
2. LIVING ROOM
3. LIBRARY
4. DINING ROOM
5. BREAKFAST ROOM
6. SCREENED PORCH
7. KITCHEN
8. FAMILY ROOM
9. BEDROOM
10. MUDROOM
11. GARAGE

KEY TO SECOND FLOOR
1. STAIR HALL
2. MASTER BEDROOM
3. MASTER BATH
4. DRESSING ROOM
5. OFFICE
6. BEDROOM

FIRST FLOOR PLAN

0 5 10   20 ft

Opposite and below
Both the covered porch and
the terrace above were
extended by five feet in depth,
creating a generous covered
seating area below and open-
air seating above with access
from two bedrooms.

Opposite

In the library, green-painted woodwork and a stone fireplace were exchanged for a muted palette and spare surfaces that deferred to the artworks. The living room communicates directly with the library through pocketing doors.

Below

With windows on three sides, the living room enjoys expansive views of Georgica Cove. Doors flanking the picture window permit easy access to the outdoors and connect the domestic interior experience to its surroundings.

Below
Like the library, the dining room was originally an octagonal room that was rationalized and enlarged to accommodate family occasions. The bay window was added to create a separate place for small-group gatherings in proximity to the view.

Opposite, above
The breakfast room, used for casual family meals, conveys the character of a glazed porch.

Opposite, below
The kitchen was enlarged and reoriented to face the pool. With direct access to the dining and breakfast rooms, the screened porch, and the family room, the kitchen presides as the center of family life.

Left and opposite
The stair and second-floor hallway remained largely the same, but we darkened the antique pine floors and handrails and lightened the walls to make the overall experience at once calmer and more graphic. Wainscoting in the seating area ties the stair landing to the surrounding spaces.

Below
The new family room, with simple paneling and beaming, a fireplace, and a bay large enough for a game table, occupies what had been a void between the service wing and garage.

Below and opposite, above
Both the master bedroom and a child's room received trim and cabinetry to give them more structure. The windows were reorganized to increase the glazing and focus on the view.

Opposite, below
In the master bath, a new freestanding tub stands on a floor finished with marble hexagonal tiles.

Opposite

In contrast to the largely monochrome palette that prevails throughout the rest of the house, pops of bright color were introduced into the grandchildren's rooms, along with playful touches like the sculptural ceiling fixtures.

Right

The game room on the basement level received a new decorative treatment but remained otherwise unchanged. We excavated space for the new screening room that adjoins it, finished in fabric panels and architectural details connecting it to the casual spaces above.

Below
The east wing overlooks
the pool and its pavilion. Each
of the three gables contains
a grandchild's room. The first-
floor covered porch serves
the kitchen and family room. The
screened porch at the end
connects to the breakfast room.

Opposite, above
A pedimented classical structure,
the new pool pavilion offers
a deep, shaded retreat from
the sun.

Opposite, below
The screened porch off the
breakfast room has a radiant-
heat floor and can be fitted
with glass panels, making it
usable in three seasons.

RESIDENCE AT WEST TISBURY

Set on eighty-five acres of forest and meadows overlooking Vineyard Sound, this tranquil retreat for a couple and their three children was conceived as a modern-day farmstead. The clients' program called for a number of structures in addition to a main house, among them a guest cottage, a pool house, a working barn, and an enclosed squash court. Working with landscape architect Rodney Robinson, we arranged them in a relaxed plan, strung along a meandering path that enhances the appreciation of the gardens and natural landscape. Though designed all at once, and unified by their material palette and scale, the house and its outbuildings suggest a fictive but uncontrived backstory of a property developed over time.

We shared our clients' vision of the main residence as a farmhouse that had been modified and added onto through the years. For precedent, we looked at houses by such architects as John Russell Pope and Mellor, Meigs & Howe, but we also referred to vernacular examples on the Vineyard, Cape Cod, and the

KEY TO COMPOUND PLAN
1. MAIN HOUSE
2. POOL AND POOL HOUSE
3. COTTAGE
4. GARAGE
5. BARN AND FARM OFFICE
6. SQUASH BARN

COMPOUND PLAN

0   50 100   200 ft

New England mainland. The house is relatively modest in scale, with a shingled center pavilion linked to two shingled wings by stone-clad hyphens. The parts are related but distinct; in keeping with the illusion of accretion, each volume is given its own local symmetries, which add a formal order to the picturesque asymmetry of the whole composition.

A gallery, generously glazed on its eastern side, runs nearly the full length of the house. Broad enough to be a functional furnished room rather than merely a passageway, it provides a layer of privacy between the principal rooms and the entry garden while encouraging an easy flow between indoors and out. Its windows also bring abundant morning light into rooms that are primarily oriented to afternoon and sunset views.

The center pavilion, which projects toward the water to offer three exposures, reflects the island's shipbuilding tradition with its three-bay porch surmounted by a bow-shaped roof. The living room occupies the gable with a high ceiling that follows the bowed roofline. A small second-floor balcony overlooks the room and views to the water. We typically select finishes that provide our rooms with texture, character, and a sense of scale. Here the living room—the formal center of the house—is the most buttoned-up with its refined Georgian detailing and its grand fireplace, while natural-finish cypress paneling and wide-plank oak floors bring the room back down to earth.

The foursquare mass and straightforward detailing of the two-story north wing—the family room below, guest bedrooms above—suggest an addition built by a more prosperous and proper later generation, with Federal-style corner pilasters supporting a simply pitched gable. In the more modest south wing, the hipped master bedroom ceiling is sheathed in flush-jointed whitewashed wood boards, almost indistinguishable from plaster but more visible and tactile as they expand and contract with the seasons. Reclaimed posts and beams—some structural, some not—are incorporated into the architecture realistically and unsentimentally, reinforcing the anecdotal nature of the house. Our objective was not so much to achieve historical accuracy as to include the sort of period details and elements that make the house a welcoming, timeless place to stay.

The outbuildings continue the narrative begun at the main house, with references to period styles and local vernacular that do not devolve into imitation, or compromise function and comfort. What appears at first glance to be a simply detailed, non-winterized beach shack is in fact a guest cottage as fully equipped and well appointed as a luxury resort bungalow. At the pool house, what looks to be a simple open-air lanai bookended by twin pavilions transforms into a comfortable living room in inclement weather with pocketing glass walls; the pavilions accommodate a kitchenette and changing rooms. The two-hundred-year-old timber frame of the working barn was brought to the site from New Hampshire. New shingle sheathing and the simple, regular spacing of the windows and horse-stall doors lend the barn an almost abstract rationalism that complements its post-and-beam skeleton.

Across a field and nestled into a rise, a second barn, newly constructed from old beams and reclaimed siding, suggests a derelict farm building that has been resurrected for a new and very specific use: it accommodates a regulation-size squash court. Like the main house, each of these secondary structures is rich in meaning, yet the full ensemble seems to have evolved naturally and inevitably, without the obvious involvement of architects.

Roger Seifter, Project Partner

KEY TO FIRST FLOOR
1. ENTRY HALL
2. LIVING ROOM
3. DINING ROOM
4. KITCHEN
5. GALLERY
6. PERGOLA
7. SCREENED PORCH
8. FAMILY ROOM
9. FAMILY STAIR
10. MUDROOM
11. STUDY
12. MASTER BEDROOM
13. MASTER BATH
14. HER DRESSING ROOM
15. HIS DRESSING ROOM

KEY TO SECOND FLOOR
1. UPPER STAIR HALL
2. BEDROOM
3. BALCONY ALCOVE

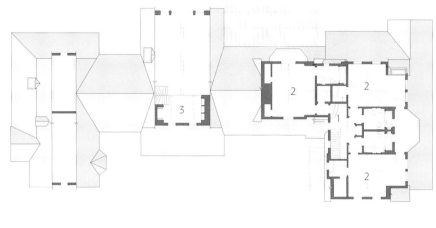

MAIN HOUSE, SECOND FLOOR PLAN

0   6   12   24 ft

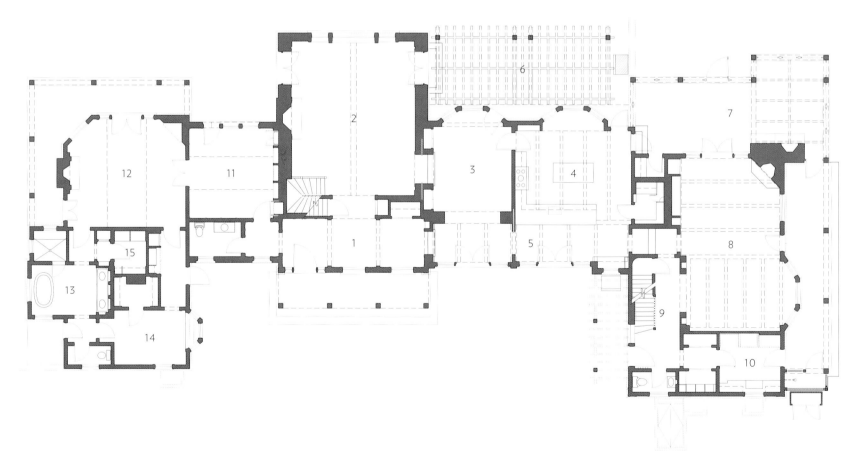

MAIN HOUSE, FIRST FLOOR PLAN

0   3   6   12 ft

Below

The entry side of the main house, seen here from the vegetable garden, is composed of three gabled and shingled pavilions connected by stone-clad hyphens.

Overleaf

From the water side the massing of the main house is even more picturesque, as wings extend at different heights and from either side of the bow-roofed living room. Children's bedrooms are within the offset double gable above the screened porch and breakfast bay; the deep pergola shades the kitchen and dining room.

Opposite, above

Paved with granite flags up to six inches thick, the breakfast terrace opens eastward off the gallery and looks across the front lawn. A pergola shelters the dutch door to the family entry.

Opposite, below

The front porch and entry, seen here across the breakfast terrace, are at a high point on the site, which gently drops away along the glazed gallery towards the kitchen and family room.

Right

The view from the dutch door at the family entry, past the breakfast terrace and front porch to a bay window in the master dressing room.

Opposite

The bow roof of the center pavilion is fully expressed in the gently arched ceiling in the living room. East-facing windows light a balcony alcove with built-in shelves; toward the water a Gothic revival arch plays against the curve of the ceiling.

Below, left

The rough stone surround of the living room fireplace is juxtaposed with a more refined and formal cypress mantelpiece.

Below, right

The dining room is set a few steps below the living room. Its blue-wash paneling and casework, wrought-iron hardware and low ceiling combine to make this the most "colonial" room in the house.

Left

A view along the gallery, past the kitchen and dining room towards the entry hall, shows the subtle change in levels as well as the interior finish palette—plaster walls, flat wood mouldings, old beams and reclaimed plank floors—at this end of the house. Extensive glazing along the east wall admits ample morning light.

Opposite

The centerpiece of the kitchen is a blue-painted working island topped by a thick antique slab of white marble. In contrast, the surrounding cabinet counter-tops are oiled pine.

Opposite, below

Double-loaded storage makes up the wall between the kitchen and gallery; a pass-through by the sink can be closed off by pocketing doors for catered events.

Opposite

The screened porch accommodates both lounge seating and dining. A long table accommodates eight near the kitchen, while comfortable sofas and armchairs occupy the adjacent gabled bay.

Right

The focal point of the seating area is a flat-faced rubble stone fireplace wall, a tour de force of the local mason's artistry. An old timber beam, supported on rubble corbels, serves as the mantel.

Opposite, above

The pine-paneled and beam-ceilinged family room is the house's "snug," nestled beyond the kitchen and behind the screened porch. Unlike most of the rooms, its focus is internal, with its river-rock fireplace and antique pool table.

Opposite, below

The screening room is fully paneled in oak and serves as a library and sitting room as well as a theater.

Right, top

The sage green beaded board paneling in the family entry combines utility with style. The wide opening to the family room offers a glimpse of the blue-painted Swedish panels sourced by interior designer Bunny Williams.

Right, center and bottom

In the second-floor hall and bedrooms, the shape and structure of the roof are fully expressed. The roof has been allowed to "interfere" with the interior so that rafters cut into head casings and some doors are chamfered. The resulting, seemingly accidental character adds to the authenticity of the house.

Below

Like most of the pitched ceilings in the house, the one in the master bedroom is paneled in re-sawn, match-jointed, and painted boards. Allowed to expand and contract with the change in seasons, their resultant craquelure adds subtly to their character.

Opposite, left

A powder room at the knuckle between the main gallery and master suite features a wainscot of flat wood planks and a faux bamboo dressing table repurposed as a vanity.

Opposite, right

At the master-bedroom fireplace, a country Federal mantelpiece is paired with an eighteenth-century Delft tile surround.

Opposite, right below

Consistent with the house's anecdotal character, the oversized windows and free-standing tub in the master bath suggest conversion of the room to its current use by some imagined past owner.

Left
The modest scale of the
poolhouse dictated its simple
form: a gabled living porch
flanked by a pair of enclosed
service spaces.

Below
Weathered shingles give
a sense of age to the poolhouse interior.

Below
The poolhouse offers a
panoramic view of Vineyard
Sound and distant islands.
Pocketed glass panels on each
side protect the sitting area
in inclement weather.

Opposite, above

The nineteenth-century frame of the barn was moved to the site from New Hampshire. At one end the barn opens onto a level grass walkout, retained against the natural slope by battered rubble walls. The adjacent, single-story farm office is newly built and houses guests and staff.

Opposite, below

The barn is a commanding presence in its landscape. An abstract profile, combined with the simple rhythms of windows and doors, gives each facade a great deal of visual power.

Right

Newly built stone walls were threaded through the natural and managed landscape as a means of suggesting order and a sense of history.

Below

The exposed frame gives the interior of the barn the same visual impact as the exterior.

Bottom

The property is dotted with seemingly random but genuinely practical architectural moments—this stone root cellar conceals electrical equipment.

Below and opposite
The main space in the farm office is an asymmetrical double-height sitting room with steps up to a sleeping loft. Old posts and beams suggest a structure in which the plaster walls are matter-of-factly treated as infill, at times set almost flush to the timbers and at others obscuring them. The sleeping loft has ample storage, thanks to built-ins under the eaves.

Opposite
The framing of the cottage was left fully exposed to create a rustic ambience. From the bedroom French doors open to a private deck overlooking Vineyard Sound.

Right
Nestled into a wooded rise overlooking the meadow, the squash barn is set into the slope to reduce the impact of the court on its exterior height and mass. Reclaimed framing timbers and old cedar siding, still mossy and stained, suggest a once-derelict structure put to a new use. A comfortable seating balcony overlooks the court.

Throughout the property there are moments for contemplation and peaceful walks, shaped by landscape architect Rodney Robinson, who shared our vision that even the most manicured areas remain informal and uncontrived.

cast in resin, Eve Kaplan, a New York artisan, finished it in gilt silver. These and other contributions—including the "octopus" beamed ceiling in our client's workspace and a "crown of thorns" beam pattern in the wine cellar, both designed by our office—collectively recall the influence of the arts and crafts movement on the shingle style projects of McKim, Mead & White and other great practitioners and connect what is a very contemporary home to its aesthetic forebears.

Throughout the project, the couple continuously challenged us to go further, to push even the most quotidian details in imaginative, unexpected directions, and we were happy to do so. The result is a picturesque home that commands its site like a castle—yet remains as elegantly detailed, and beautifully hand crafted, as a Fabergé egg.

Randy Correll, Project Partner

Above
This house on Fishers Island, which we designed in the 1980s for a similarly dramatic site, has a narrow plan with views in both directions. It served as a starting point for the Buzzards Bay residence.

Overleaf
On the exposed site, a stone wall protects the pool and its pergola from the strong prevailing winds.

Left and bottom
The negative-edge pool seems to spill directly into Buzzards Bay. The redwood pergola shades a sitting area and spa. The pool terrace is finished in a Jerusalem stone that is light in tone and cool to the feet.

Center
At the western end of the house, a shaded porch off the living room faces southwest.

This view, with its dormers, bracketed balcony and bell-shaped roof form, is a catalogue of the house's varying shapes and volumes. The monumental stair connects the main floor to the lawn.

Below
The guest house was built first, to enable the family to visit the site while construction of the main house was underway. The two second-floor guest suites enjoy inset covered porches. The gazebo, with its bell-shaped roof at the corner, has the most prominent view of Buzzards Bay.

Opposite, above
A broad bluestone entry court-yard is a protected area for entertaining on windy days.

Opposite, below left
The guest house seen from the second-floor oriel window.

Opposite, below right
The beamed mudroom outside the kitchen features a mosaic tile floor.

Opposite and below
Beyond the stone surround of the entry porch, a sunflower-inspired transom and stained-glass side lights panels frame the front door. The stained-glass panels were inspired by originals our client discovered in Venice. Playful dolphin brackets perch upon stone corbels at the front porch.

Left and below
The semi-enclosed octagonal
breakfast room is open to both
the kitchen and family room.

Opposite
The kitchen, with its two
islands, communicates directly
with the family room and
bar/pantry.

Right and opposite, bottom
The beams add texture and interest to the living room's architecture and help to bring down the scale of what is a very large room. The archway at right leads to the library, bar and back stair. The distinctive interlocking circle motif in the windows is adapted from a house on Fisher's Island.

Left
The master office, with its panoramic view of Buzzards Bay from the top of the tower, features a beam system we referred to as "the octopus."

Below
The back stair wall, crafted by the Martha's Vineyard mason Lew French, includes a keystone archway (leading to the library), an interior fountain surrounded by an old well cover, and granite slabs that echo the progression of the steps.

Opposite
French also crafted the library fireplace, which interleaves beach stones and driftwood. The bordered walnut floor and bowed mahogany wall boards demanded precise carpentry.

Below
With water views on two sides
and no foreground of land,
the master bedroom feels as if
it is floating above the sea.
The mantel, a fantasia of shells
and seaweed, was cast in resin
and silver-leafed.

Opposite, left
The floor and vaulted ceiling
in the master bath were
executed in teak. The blue
marble wainscoting was
selected for its evocation
of water.

Opposite, right
In the guest rooms, we took
advantage of the roofline
to create interestingly shaped
and articulated ceilings.

Opposite, top
The stone wall lining the back stair continues down to the lower level, where an archway leads to the wine room, with an interlocking 'crown of thorns' beam motif.

Opposite, bottom
The game room features a remarkable example of craft: a boat-shaped bar with a "hull" copied from a type of boat made locally in South Dartmouth.

Right and below
The rubblestone base of screened cabana off the pool area extends inside as a fireplace with a mantel of driftwood found on a nearby beach.

HOUSE AT GLEN ELLEN

Sonoma County, in northern California, is distinct in character from Napa, its better-known neighbor: the hilly, intimate landscape, with beautiful winding roads, is for me one of the most sublime settings in the American landscape. Our clients, a couple for whom we have designed both a primary residence in San Francisco and a pied-à-terre in New York, had a house built for them in the 1970s on a twenty-acre site—a spectacular location on a ridge of land that drops off into valleys on three sides, with a view of Sonoma Mountain to the south. When a neighboring property became available, the couple asked if I'd visit and give them my thoughts on its potential.

The building site, on the high point of the adjacent land, roughly a quarter-mile from their house, offered 270-degree views across Sonoma Valley toward Napa to the east and Sugarloaf Mountain to the north, vistas quite different from those offered by their existing house site. There was also a pool cottage down the slope, on a more secluded location on the property, and the

Opposite
The porch of the Poet's Room at the Ahwahnee, the hilltop retreat in northern California, captures a view of the hills near Sonoma Mountain. Inspired by the work of Bernard Maybeck, the porch features overscaled architectural elements, notably the "board-and-batten" piers and an exposed truss. The red window trim, a color suggested by interior designer Agnes Bourne, reappears in the main house and two outbuildings, helping to tie together the five structures on the property.

KEY TO COMPOUND PLAN
1. AHWAHNEE
2. POOL COTTAGE
3. GARAGE
4. GYM
5. MAIN HOUSE

COMPOUND PLAN

0   30   60   120 ft

two sites complemented, and contrasted with, one another. Our clients were understandably concerned that the hilltop location might feel too exposed. I suggested the site was appealing for precisely that reason: it offered a counterpoint to their existing residence and, together with the pool house, would create an unusual variety of topographical experiences—and an equal variety of views.

On the hilltop, the couple envisioned a writer's retreat and a place for alfresco entertaining, which they named the Ahwahnee after the legendary National Park Service lodge in Yosemite, a favorite of theirs. For inspiration, we drew on the work of California architects Bernard Maybeck and William Wurster, and the vernacular barn and shed buildings found throughout the region. The principal models, however, were a Frank Lloyd Wright project, and the gardener's cottage by Karl Friedrich Schinkel in Potsdam featuring two symmetrically related pavilions separated by a terrace. We designed a U-shaped composition with an open-air dining terrace framed by pergolas, an enclosed structure— named the Poet's Room—with an almost identical footprint and an expanse of green lawn serving as an "oasis" between them.

Crucial to the design's success is the element of surprise. Approaching from the motor court, one sees what appears to be two farm buildings accessed via a pair of large sliding barn doors— a blind wall offering no hint of what is to come. Opening the doors reveals a view across the green carpet of lawn to a vista of mountains and valleys beyond, framed by the al-fresco dining area to the right, and the Poet's Room at left. The flagstone-paved dining area features over-scaled pergola members supported by four "board-and-batten order" piers; the Poet's Room— created in collaboration with interior designer Agnes Bourne—is dominated by a Bernard Maybeck inspired tapering poured-in-place concrete fireplace on axis with a broad bay window and rising some fifteen feet to a peaked, robustly cedar paneled ceiling. Wide pocket doors on opposite sides of the room open to frame a cross-axial view, terminating in a stone fireplace beside the dining pergola to the west and, to the east, the pool pavilion below. Perhaps not as grand as its namesake in Yosemite, this Ahwahnee rides its hilltop with a quiet classical eloquence.

The pool cottage offers a contrastingly intimate, enclosed experience. While the architectural language is similar to the Ahwahnee's, the relationship between the interior and exterior spaces is quite different, with the structure adjoining and opening onto the pool area, and the pergola, deployed in a modified L-shape, uniting the two zones. Similarly, the small one-bedroom cottage shares the simple, carefully wrought details of its hilltop companion, but, instead of the rich

Top, left
The Ahwahnee features the Poet's Room and an open dining area shaded by a pergola with an "oasis" of green between the two.

Top, right
The Fagan house by Bernard Maybeck. with its attached pergolas and an arched window, embodies some of the elements at play in the Glen Ellen buildings.

Above
The original Ahwahnee, a landmark National Park Service lodge at Yosemite, California, a favorite of our client, influenced the spirit of this project.

reds and natural wood tones of the Ahwahnee, the interior is almost pure white as a quiet backdrop for the pool. The sense of privacy, presence of water, and interplay between sunshine and shadow give the pool cottage its own special character.

Not too long after these two structures were completed, the main house suffered from seismic activity, which had damaged the structure beyond repair. I counseled my clients to build a new group of buildings: the main house and two ancillary buildings. The red-painted cedar house, located beyond a gateway formed by pavilions housing a gym and a garage, is volumetrically playful, a response to the surrounding topography and mountains. It was conceived to suggest an existing barn-and-silo arrangement that had additional elements appended over time. The "silo," a two-story octagonal form, serves as the entry hall and stair tower and is a hinge between the public rooms and expansive master suite. Its chamfered corners also focus the interior views, drawing the eye diagonally across the living room from the front door to the large west-facing window and pool terrace beyond.

This project afforded an unusual opportunity: to use familiar compositional elements and deploy them in different combinations, at multiple scales, and with varying degrees of emphasis, across five distinct structures: board-and-batten, corrugated metal, articulated pillars and trellises, as well as specific colors and materials, all working together to bring continuity to a multiplicity of experiences. This continuity, moreover, extends to all of the work we have designed for this client. As they move from place to place, everything remains comfortable and familiar—the circumstances may change, but the two are always at home.

Grant Marani, Project Partner

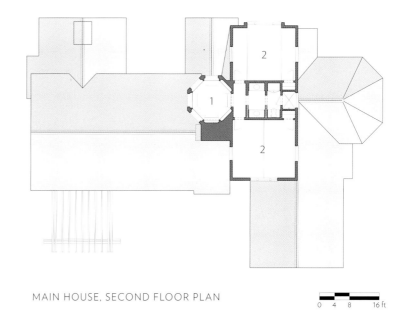

Opposite

The composition of the main house drew on Karl Friedrich Schinkel's court gardener's house at Potsdam, while individual architectural components owe more to California architects Bernard Maybeck and William Wurster. In the narrative developed for the house, we envisioned a silo-and-barn farm building to which additions were made over time.

MAIN HOUSE, SECOND FLOOR PLAN

0 4 8   16 ft

KEY TO FIRST FLOOR
1. ENTRY PORCH
2. ENTRY HALL
3. LIVING/DINING ROOM
4. KITCHEN
5. GALLERY
6. OFFICE
7. SUNROOM
8. MASTER BEDROOM
9. MASTER BATH
10. DRESSING ROOM
11. TERRACE

KEY TO SECOND FLOOR
1. SITTING ROOM
2. BEDROOM

MAIN HOUSE, FIRST FLOOR PLAN

0 4 8   16 ft

Opposite and right

The entrance drive passes between the gym and garage buildings, which acknowledge the arrangement of volumes found at the hilltop Ahwahnee but with the gables now perpendicularly arranged. The buildings introduce multiple elements that comprise the aesthetic language of the complex: board-and-batten siding, trellises, bold trusswork, and corrugated metal roofing. The use of the color red, which appears in four of the five structures, begins here. A dark stain on the cedar siding suggests a weathered finish.

Overleaf

The playful asymmetrical composition includes a small shed, which contains the kitchen entrance, a Maybeck-inspired arched window, and a barbecue-and-pergola arrangement similar to the one at the Ahwahnee.

Opposite

The master suite is on the
ground floor in the projecting
wing at right; guest bedrooms
are on the second floor. The
structure atop the chimney,
known as the "doghouse," closely
resembles an element in the
primary residence we designed
for the couple in San Francisco.

Below

A canopy of woven twigs
suggested by interior designer
Agnes Bourne shades the
dining porch and infuses the
space with an ever-changing
pattern of dappled sunlight.

Opposite

The east-facing sunroom captures abundant morning light through a large bay window. The asymmetrical composition includes a Juliet balcony off the master bedroom.

Below

The entrance porch, with its large Sonoma field stone piers, is set on axis with the octagonal tower, which sits atop the octagonal entrance vestibule.

Below, left
A magnificent live oak framed by the entrance porch.

Below, right
The hallway between the entrance hall and the sunroom is in effect a gallery for artwork and books.

Opposite, above left and below
The large arched window at the dining end of the great room allows beautiful western light to penetrate deep into this space. The dining room opens directly onto the dining porch through pocket doors. The sitting area also has large pocket doors on both north and south sides of the room. The fireplace surround is made of regional kiln tiles.

Opposite, above right
The kitchen, which opens directly to the dining area, can be closed off with mirrored pocket doors. Triangular clerestory windows inject a modern note to both the interior and exterior.

Below and opposite
At the entrance to the
Ahwahnee, sliding barn doors
open to an expanse of lawn
flanked by the Poet's Room
and dining pergola and an
incomparably dramatic vista.
The configuration of the
Ahwahnee's volumes is similar
to the relationship between
the garage and gym, while the
symmetrical connection
between the dining pergola
and Poet's Room replicates
the configuration of the dining
porch and master suite at the
main house.

Opposite, left
The Ahwahnee's primary kitchen is adjacent to the dining pergola; this kitchenette, bathed in Maybeck-inspired red, is off the Poet's Room.

Opposite, right
In the Poet's Room, a poured-in-place concrete fireplace rises to meet the diagonal cedar boards of the ceiling, the two materials elegantly complementing one another.

Right
The bay in the Poet's Room opens onto a shaded porch; the window is similar to one in the couple's master bedroom in San Francisco.

Right, below
An axial view through the open pocket-doors of the Poet's Room across the lawn to the dining pergola.

Opposite

The pool cottage is a simple gabled structure with four sets of French doors, three of them shaded by a pergola supported by robust board-and-batten piers. Beyond are the doors to the bedroom.

Below

The interior of the pool cottage is finished in a bright, fresh white. Maybeck-inspired arched window in the bedroom captures abundant light, while glazed sliding doors in the dressing room open up to the landscape to the north.

RESIDENCE IN EAST QUOGUE

The design of this residence, on a dune overlooking Long Island's south shore, presented an unusual creative challenge, one that involved reinterpreting the historic regional shingle style that our office had helped to revive some thirty years ago.

Our clients, a couple with two teenage children, purchased the rare double oceanfront lot for its location and views, but without a specific notion of the sort of house that would best suit them. In the course of developing design studies, I took them to a shingle style home, not far from their own site, which the office had completed in the mid-1980s. They responded immediately and positively to the plan and scale, and very specifically to the style of architecture. This was not surprising. Though only one of a parade of styles that found favor between the 1880s and 1930s, the shingled house's associations with a casual way of summer living have made it enduringly appealing. Ever since our office returned it to prominence on eastern Long Island more than a generation ago, examples have proliferated. Therein lay the rub:

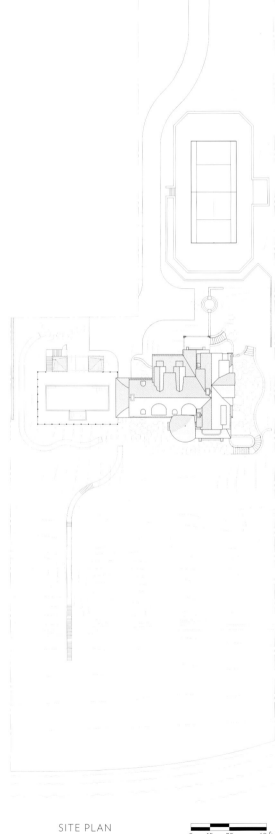

SITE PLAN

0 15 30   60 ft

watered-down "developer special" shingle houses were everywhere throughout the area and adding to the brown-shingled parade seemed akin to a failure of imagination.

I have always been a fan of the Queen Anne style shingle residences around Providence, as well as the houses and casinos completed by McKim, Mead & White in Newport, and I decided to reinvestigate these precedents. Doing so, I was struck by the remarkable richness of detail, the Gilded Age flair and exuberance, animating both the private and public structures of that time. There is something thrilling, poignant, and, indeed, optimistic about them, the way the architecture's decorative extravagance conjures up an idyllic American past filled with blue skies, colorful regattas, the snap of flags and sails. What could distinguish the couple's house from its brethren, we believed, was a comparable measure of richness, shot through as it was with joy.

The plan itself is relatively uncomplicated: L-shaped, with an enfilade of main-floor public rooms looking across the dunes to the ocean and a master suite and two children's bedrooms on the second floor. Though the ocean-facing south elevation is at grade with the dunes, the site drops abruptly on the east side, allowing a lower level, in which we set three additional bedrooms, and an expansive game and media space known as the summer room.

Because of height restrictions, we located the second floor in the residence's gambrel roof; inserting dormers into the shaped ceilings in a way that brought in light and maximized views proved to be the design's great brain-twister. Fortuitously, in balancing the internal programmatic needs and exterior aesthetics, we were aided by the shingle style itself, which exchanges symmetry for a rambling picturesqueness.

Ironically, the element that makes the living spaces in this traditional house so grand is very modern: the enormous windows framing the panoramic ocean vistas. Though a historic shingle residence would never have had glazing of this scale, big windows do appear in shingle style public buildings, such as resorts and clubhouses, from the period. Here we chose to blend the two, by adding window sticking around the perimeters of the large panes, which introduces enough contrast to convey a sense of historic appropriateness yet preserves the sweeping water and dune views.

We took a consistent approach with the architectural detail: for every element, we began by designing what might be considered the norm for a shingle house, then asked ourselves how it might be reinterpreted while still remaining stylistically accurate. On the exterior, this is manifest in the Gothic bed moulding and lively combinations of diamond and fish-scale shingles that animate the surface. Unusual interpretative elements include the trellis design derived from sailing knots, the copper pine cone finial on the circular dining porch, and the custom globe-shaped lantern adorned with the points of the compass suspended from the porch ceiling. This approach extends to the exterior color palette, in which the shingled wrapper of Cape Cod gray is offset by teal shutters and window members painted a gray-blue.

Opposite
The house occupies a privileged site, a double lot between the Atlantic and Shinnecock Bay, and takes advantage of views in both directions.

Top
The dining porch and field-stone-paved terrace face a lawn of dune plantings and, beyond it, the ocean.

Above
McKim, Mead & White's festive casino in Newport, Rhode Island, which opened in 1880, served as a design inspiration.

Certain of the exterior elements, such as the arched openings and oceanside color scheme, were carried indoors. But the vitality of the rooms derives in large measure from the expression of the boards of the walls and ceilings, the variety of their combination and multidirectional design. Every room and transitional space has its particular logic, and all are different. Rather than feeling excessive, this tectonic accretion gives the house scale, rhythm, and, not least, interest. There is always something to discover, a detail or combination previously unseen.

We also sought to give the house a proper context, selectively re-grading the site and inserting retaining walls to craft a palette of outdoor experiences. These include the path that circles up from the motor court through a garden to the entry porch steps; a side garden, with rough-cut stone pavers off the summer room, featuring a colorful palette of summer flowers; and the lawn of dune grass, through which winds an irregular wood-slatted walkway leading to the beach. The landscaping veils the neighboring structures, and the interior plan deliberately shapes view corridors that capture the natural environment.

Gary Brewer, Project Partner

Opposite

The house and adjoining pool sit between a pea gravel motor court and the rear lawn. The master suite and children's bedrooms fill the dutch gambrel roof and dormers; the roofscape suggests the complexity of fitting in all the second-floor rooms.

Overleaf

The view from the guest house of the main residence, the pool and its cabana, and the ocean beyond.

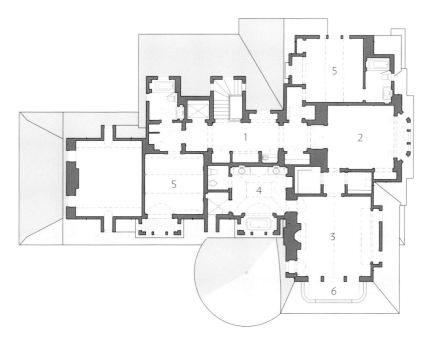

SECOND FLOOR PLAN

0 4 8   16 ft

KEY TO FIRST FLOOR
1. ENTRY PORCH
2. ENTRY HALL
3. LIBRARY
4. LIVING ROOM
5. DINING ROOM
6. KITCHEN
7. FAMILY ROOM
8. SOUTH PORCH
9. DINING PORCH
10. POOL PORCH
11. POOL CANABA

KEY TO SECOND FLOOR
1. UPPER STAIR HALL
2. SITTING ROOM
3. MASTER BEDROOM
4. MASTER BATH
5. BEDROOM
6. TERRACE

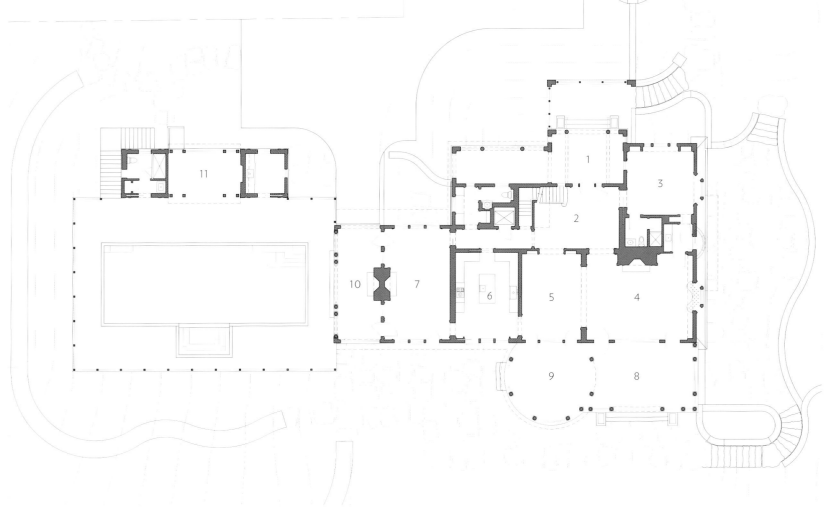

FIRST FLOOR PLAN

0 4 8   16 ft

Below
At the base of the three-story
side elevation is a media and
game room (called the summer
room). Broad stone steps lead
up to the front porch.

*Opposite, clockwise
from upper left*
The rafter-tail ends of the pool
cabana pergola: a trellis design
based on sailing knots beneath
a Gothic bed moulding; the
library window, with shutters,
window hood, and custom
flower box; the dining porch roof,
with its custom copper finial;
the entry porch, with its stone
piers and painted Doric columns;
a custom side light, with glass
rondels, beside the front door.

Opposite

In the entry hall, to the left of the main stair the large arched opening connects to the dining room.

Opposite, below right

The fluted top and paneled shaft of the pilasters at the arched opening between the entry hall and living and dining rooms.

Opposite, below left

The entry porch, looking toward the library window. The joints of the stone piers, handrails, and clapboard provide an ever-changing play of shadows.

Below

The pin-stripe design of the wall boarding alternates a white-painted beaded board with flat boards of red oak finished in a beige-grey. The two arches leading to the living and dining rooms create an open flow from the entry hall and a direct ocean view.

Below
The living room seating groups arranged around the fireplace were developed by interior designer Stephen Gambrel. Large windows and doors open to the panoramic ocean view.

Opposite
A large cased archway frames the opening between the living and dining rooms. The pocket door to the left opens to the kitchen.

Opposite, below
From the living room, openings lead to the dining room, entry hall, and bar, with the library beyond. The window seat in the bay is a cozy place to escape with a book. Translucent window panes, reminiscent of the color of seashells, soften the view of the neighbors.

Right and below
The kitchen combines a traditional aesthetic with a contemporary level of comfort and utility. The soft grey hand-painted finish on the cabinets and glazed wall tiles evoke seashells and driftwood.

Far right
The design of the dining room buffet draws on the treatment of the windows and its woven trellises.

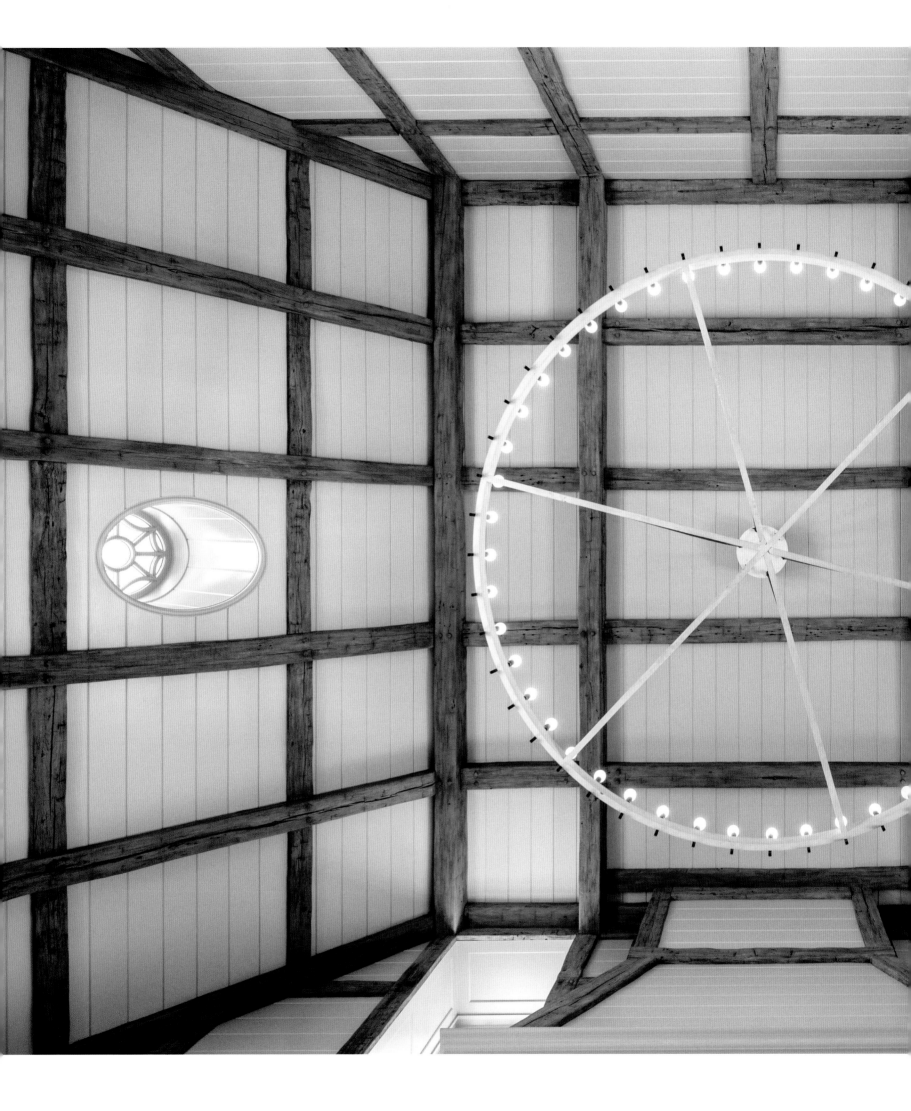

Opposite, top and below left
In the library, antiqued oak walls are paired with a plaster ceiling overlaid with a Chinoiserie fretwork. A wall sculpture by Louise Nevelson relates to the geometry and color of the ceiling.

Opposite, below right
The second-floor stair landing features a shallow vaulted ceiling and enfilade of arched cased openings.

Below
The master sitting room, at the end of the second-floor hall, continues the vault-and-beam motif. Above the window seat a diamond-patterned window combines milk glass and transparent panes.

Below
In the master bedroom, a boat-like bow ceiling sits within a dutch gambrel roof. The antique mirror above the fireplace conceals a TV; beyond the expansive Palladian window, a small balcony faces the ocean.

Opposite
In the master bathroom, a dressing table stands between twin vanities. The pattern in the floor and doors brings in the "woven" motif found throughout the interior and exterior details of the house. The tub sits in an alcove with a view over the dining room porch roof, while the elliptical window in the shower looks toward the ocean.

Opposite
An ocean-facing window seat alcove in one of the children's rooms is the width of a double bed, an ideal situation for sleepovers.

Below
An operable elliptical window in a second-floor stair hall alcove.

Right
The stair rises within a dormer topped by an arched window featuring a Gothic fan light.

Below, right
A tub alcove in one of the children's bathrooms is set into a dormer with an arched Gothic window looking toward Shinnecock Bay.

Opposite

In a child's bedroom, the shaped ceiling follows the form of the gambrel roof. The playful swag detail, which gives the banquette alcove the flavor of a proscenium, draws on a Swedish precedent.

Below

The ground-level Summer Room, which opens to the side garden, serves as a game and media room and as a casual communal space for the bedrooms that open to it.

Below
The round dining porch is enriched with a lively pattern of exposed rafters and a "globe" chandelier.

Opposite
Amenities at the pool include a cabana and a generous pool porch just outside the family room. A fireplace extends the use of pool porch into the cooler weather. Bow-shaped rafters and a nautical-themed trellis connect the space to the dunes and pool.

PROJECT CREDITS

HOUSE ON LAKE MICHIGAN
Partner: Randy M. Correll
Project Associate: Timothy S. Deal
Project Assistants: Glenn Albrecht, Haven
Knight, Samuel O'Meara, Mark Rodriguez,
David Vimont, Holly Zeiler
Interior Designer: Victoria Hagan Interiors
Landscape Architect: Hoerr Schaudt Landscape Architects

RESIDENCE ON BEL AIR ROAD, LOS ANGELES, CALIFORNIA
Partner: Roger H. Seifter
Project Senior Associate: Victoria Baran
Project Senior Assistant: Christopher McIntire
Project Assistants: Alexander Butler,
Susanna Chao, Joshua Coleman, Troy Curry,
Timothy S. Deal, Caroline Graf Statile, Sallie
Hambright, Joshua Lekwa, Todd Sullivan
Interior Designer: Thomas Pheasant
Landscape Project Managers: Ashley Christopher,
Bibi Gaston
Landscape Design Assistant: Mark Rodriguez

RESIDENCE IN HIGHLAND PARK, ILLINOIS
Partner: Grant F. Marani
Project Senior Associate: Charles Toothill
Project Associates: Rosa Maria Colina,
Megan St. Denis
Project Assistants: Peter Lombardi,
Mark Pledger, Zong Ji Zhan
Interior Designer: Semel Snow Interior Design
Landscape Architect: Hoerr Schaudt
Landscape Architects

SEASIDE COTTAGE, SEASIDE, FLORIDA
Partner: Gary L. Brewer
Project Manager: Mark Pledger
Project Assistants: Kayin Tse, Kim Yap;
Interior Design Associate: Ken Stuckenschneider
Interior Design Assistant: Georgette Sturam
Landscape Design Project Managers: Ashley
Christopher, Mei Wu
Landscape Design Assistant: Jennifer Berlly

ENCINAL BLUFFS FAMILY COMPOUND, MALIBU, CALIFORNIA
Partner: Roger H. Seifter
Associate Partner: Arthur Chabon
Project Associates: Jacob Morrison,
David Solomon
Project Assistants: Hyuna Chung, Thomas
Fletcher, Dennis Giobbe, Henry Gunawan,
Lenore Passavanti, George Punnoose,
Corina Rugeroni, Lynn Wang, Daniel Wolfskehl
Interior Designers: Kenyon Kramer and
Jean-Louis Raynaud; Atelier AM
Landscape Designer: Deborah Nevins & Associates
Associate Architect: A. Thomas Torres Architects

MAISONETTE IN CHICAGO, ILLINOIS
Partner: Randy M. Correll
Project Manager: Craig Stevens
Project Assistant: Allen Philip Robinson
Interior Designer: Arthur Dunnam, Jed Johnson Associates

HOUSE ON HOOK POND, EAST HAMPTON, NEW YORK
Partner: Randy M. Correll
Project Manager: Timothy S. Deal
Project Assistant: Alexis M. Ryder

RESIDENCE IN NAPA COUNTY, OAKVILLE, CALIFORNIA
Partner: Roger H. Seifter
Project Managers: Victoria Baran, Robert Epley
Project Assistants: Elise Geiger, Dennis Giobbe
Interior Designer: Eugenia Jesberg, EJ Interior Design
Landscape Architects: Dennis McGlade, OLIN

HOUSE AT BLUE WATER HILL, WESTPORT, CONNECTICUT
Partner: Gary L. Brewer
Project Managers: Maryann Kril, Lenore Passavanti
Project Assistants: Lauren Cahill, Katie Casanta
Rasmussen, Brendan Lee
Interior Designer: Arthur Dunnam, Jed Johnson Associates;
Jennifer Gresinger Interior Design
Landscape Design Associate: Michael Weber

WEST VILLAGE TOWNHOUSE,
NEW YORK, NEW YORK
Partner: Randy M. Correll
Project Associate: Rosa Maria Colina
Project Manager: Caroline Graf Statile
Project Assistants: Matt Casey,
Nicholas DeRosa, Michael Dudley,
Josh Lekwa, Jeremy Shannon
Interior Designer: Courtney Phillips Stern
Landscape Design Project Manager:
Ashley Christopher

HOUSE ON GEORGICA COVE,
EAST HAMPTON, NEW YORK
Partner: Randy M. Correll
Project Manager: Lenore Passavanti
Project Assistants: Nicholas Azevedo,
Hannah Cho, Sho Okajima, Allen Philip
Robinson, Hilary Tate
Interior Designer: David Kleinberg Design Associates
Landscape Architect: Edmund D. Hollander
Landscape Architect Design P.C.

RESIDENCE AT WEST TISBURY,
MARTHA'S VINEYARD, MASSACHUSETTS
Partners: Randy M. Correll,
Roger H. Seifter
Project Associates: Josh Bull,
Catherine Popple
Senior Project Assistants: Thomas Morbitzer
Project Assistant: Christopher McIntire
Interior Designer: Bunny Williams Inc.
Squash Barn Interior Designer: John Gilmer
Landscape Architect: Rodney Robinson
Landscape Architects

HOUSE ON BUZZARDS BAY,
SOUTH DARTMOUTH, MASSACHUSETTS
Partner: Randy M. Correll
Project Manager: Damon Van Horne
Project Assistants: Aaron Boucher, Anthony
Furino, Christiane Gallois, Douglas Neri,
Marc Rehman
Interior Designer: Anne Mullin Interiors
Landscape Architect: Oehme Van Sweden

HOUSE AT GLEN ELLEN,
CALIFORNIA
Partner: Grant F. Marani
Project Manager: Danny Chiang
Project Associate: Megan St. Denis
Project Assistants: Lauren Bollettino, Esther Park
Interior Designer: Agnes Bourne
Landscape Design Senior Associate: Kendra Taylor
Landscape Design Assistant: Terrie Gamble

FOLLY AND POOL COTTAGE,
GLEN ELLEN, CALIFORNIA
Partner: Grant F. Marani
Project Manager: Mark Pledger
Project Senior Assistant: Rebecca Post
Project Assistants: Catherine Dayal,
Elise Geiger, Qu Kim
Interior Designer: Agnes Bourne
Landscape Architects: Suzman and Cole Design
Associates; Ron Herman Landscape Architect

RESIDENCE IN EAST QUOGUE,
NEW YORK
Partner: Gary L. Brewer
Project Manager: Winnie Yen
Project Assistants: Katie Casanta Rasmussen,
Nicholas DeRosa, C. Callaway Hayles,
Scott Hirshson
Interior Designer: Steven Gambrel, S.R. Gambrel, Inc.
Landscape Architect: Edmund D. Hollander
Landscape Architect Design P.C.

PHOTOGRAPHY CREDITS

All photography by Peter Aaron / OTTO
except as noted below:

Courtesy AIA Archives: 82 *(bottom)*
Courtesy Berger-Levrault, Paris: 199 *(left)*
Steven Brooke: 319; Courtesy of
Architectural Digest, © 1989
California Coastal Commission: 20 *(top)*, 133
Courtesy Environmental Design Archives,
University of California, Berkeley: 343 *(top right)*
Reinhard Görner: 344 *(left)*
Courtesy Hennessey & Ingalls: 199 *(center)*
Carol M. Highsmith: 343 *(bottom)*
Erich Lessing: 103 *(bottom)*
Courtesy Library of Congress: 287
Courtesy McGraw Hill Book Company: 249 *(right)*
Courtesy Mellor, Meigs & Howe Collection,
Athenaeum of Philadelphia: 53
Hans Namuth: 16 *(center)*
Sebastian Niedlich: 103 *(center)*
Peter McCoy Construction: 55
Greg Premru: 13 *(top)*, 16 *(bottom)*
Ben Ritter: 8
Noah Sheldon: 27
Robert A.M. Stern Architects: 16 *(top)*, 131, 161,
182, 265 *(top)*, 369 *(bottom)*
Edmund Stoecklein: 17 *(bottom)*
Heinz Theuerkauf: 81 *(bottom)*
Stefen Turner: 105, 223, 224, 368, 370